PERFECT PHRASES™

for

WRITING

COMPANY

ANNOUNCEMENTS

**Hundreds of Ready-to-Use Phrases for Powerful
Internal and External Communications**

Linda Eve Diamond and Harriet Diamond

New York   Chicago   San Francisco   Lisbon   London   Madrid   Mexico City
Milan   New Delhi   San Juan   Seoul   Singapore   Sydney   Toronto

Library of Congress Cataloging-in-Publication Data

Diamond, Linda Eve.
    Perfect phrases for writing company announcements / by Linda Eve Diamond
and Harriet Diamond.
        p.   cm—(Perfect phrases).
    ISBN-13: 978-0-07-163452-6
    ISBN-10: 0-07-163452-5
    1. Business announcements.   2. Business communication.   I. Diamond,
Harriet.   II. Title.

    HF5718.D572   2010
    808′.06665—dc22   2009054325

1 2 3 4 5 6 7 8 9 10 11 12 13 14 15 16 17   WFR/WFR   1 9 8 7 6 5 4 3 2 1 0

ISBN 978-0-07-163452-6
MHID   0-07-163452-5

McGraw-Hill books are available at special quantity discounts to use as premiums and
sales promotions or for use in corporate training programs. To contact a representative,
please e-mail us at bulksales@mcgraw-hill.com.

Contents

Contents

Contents

Chapter 13: Write On!   197

Conclusion   207

Resources   209

Acknowledgments

Our thanks, as always, to Donya Dickerson and our other *perfect* editors at McGraw-Hill, Gigi Grajdura and Alison Shurtz, and to Grace Freedson's Publishing Network for introducing us to McGraw-Hill's Perfect Phrases series.

Introduction

*P*erfect Phrases for Writing Company Announcements is your personal guide to both external and internal written communication. Announcements should be phrased with care whether they're written for clients, customers, investors, employees, or anyone else who has a stake in your business or an interest in your products or services. A well-crafted announcement can inform, inspire, motivate, entice, sell, and even shape (or shape shift) your company's image.

Announce big news, but announce the small news, too, and consider making regular announcements. Keeping your name and news visible will help you stay in the consumer's mind, and regular announcements to employees will make them feel valued and worth the time and effort to be kept apprised. Sending timely, regular announcements is a tough job, but information access is constant, 24/7, and consumer attention is scattered. The more you put out new information or reminders, even in the smallest tidbits, and the more media choices you use, the more your business name will be recalled by busy minds.

When faced with writing so many company announcements, you may need the perfect phrase in a hurry—and we're here to help with hundreds of *perfect phrases* and the means to keep *perfect phrasing* in mind as you develop and refine new announcements over time.

Who Can Use This Book?

Writing, editing, and proofreading are specialized skills. However, in most small companies and in many larger ones, the job of writing company updates, announcements, and press releases often falls on the shoulders of those who are already carrying heavy loads and are forced to fit the job of promotional writer into "spare" time. Whether you work for a large or small company or you're self-employed, if you are charged with creating written announcements, you'll want to use *Perfect Phrases for Writing Company Announcements.*

Book Map

Part One Sharing Information: The Whys and Hows

Part One covers announcement basics of message and style, from media choices to language matters. These opening chapters explain why you want to get your message out, touch on choices for delivering varied messages to multiple audiences, and offer ideas about how and why to target to your audience and make your messages pop, flow, deliver, and best represent the image you want to project.

Part Two The Perfect Phrase

In Part Two, which comprises the bulk of the book, you will find perfect phrases and the mindsets behind them. Although many of our phrases could apply to multiple situations, we also offer a variety of phrases that would suit specific businesses and circumstances. Many can be altered to fit your needs; others will serve as models. As with all other *Perfect Phrases* books, the phrases may be the perfect fit or a springboard to your own perfect phrase. The more specific you are, the stronger, more meaningful, and more lasting your message will be.

Part Three Writing *Your* Perfect Phrases

Whether tweaking our phrases for your unique needs or writing an announcement on a topic not covered here, a few writing basics can help you. We provide two closing chapters to help you create and refine your own phrases and company announcements. Learn what makes a phrase perfect and find suggestions for brainstorming, creating, and evaluating effective announcement phrasing. Even with hundreds of perfect phrases in your hand, you will still need to create, refine, or even translate specialized messages at times. In the two concluding chapters, you'll find quick tips on crafting phrases, avoiding pitfalls, and polishing the final look of your announcement.

Enter Here

Perfect Phrases for Writing Announcements is an easy-to-carry, easily referenced resource for anyone who must write company announcements. Whatever your business, whatever your goals, both your image and your relationships are essential elements of your success. What do you announce and how? What is the image and style of your company that you want the world to see? What's your relationship with clients and employees, and how can you maintain contact, inform, excite, motivate, and inspire? If you're ready to make an announcement, enter here.

Part One

Sharing Information: The Whys and Hows

We are inundated with information, announcements, and advertisements. From the morning news to the ads and announcements we see and hear all day that stretch from the information superhighway to highways we drive—from billboards to bumper stickers, everyone's announcing something. How do you make your message stand out? You have to be in the right place at the right time, in just the right eye-catching way, and, of course, it helps to have the perfect phrase. The following two chapters address the basics of media choice, audience, and style.

Chapter 1

Your Message

"I will be so brief I have already finished."
—Complete text of a speech
given by Salvador Dali

The first thing to consider when crafting your announcement is your ideal audience. The more you can visualize who that might be and what's most important to them, the more you will be able to appeal to that audience in a style and on a level that speaks to its interests and needs. The second consideration is your media choice, which also might affect the style and phrasing of your message. Whatever your message and your media, remember this: *Words are forever. Use them wisely.*

Media Choices

Media choices are continually expanding and increasing in speed and accessibility. Where do you post announcements? Do you blog, update through social networking sites, or send newsletters or regular e-mail updates? Do you send press releases the old-fashioned way to the newspaper or through online PR sites, and if so, which level do you choose? Where is your intended audience most likely to look for announcements from you? Where are you most likely to capture the attention of your target audience? Even online, you need to choose from among a myriad of choices. Will you use the written word? Video? Audio? Is your announcement newsworthy enough for a press release? Is it so newsworthy that a reporter might be interested in running a feature? What is your advertising budget? Should you have a public newsletter and/or an employee newsletter? How often should it be issued? Should you run special editions for key events and announcements?

As you continue to refine your messages, remember to always be assessing your media choices. The most effective media choices may be changing at a rapid pace, so be careful not to lock in to one method, and don't be afraid to try new things. Some once-popular networking sites have fallen off as other sites have been more responsive to user needs and more forward thinking in terms of helping people find or maintain connections. For instance, one site that was extremely popular and was even used by many as a main website is now frustrating to most because of a lack of security on the site and slow-loading pages. While maintaining a page on that site may have been impressive at one time, companies that keep pace have either moved on or, at the very least, don't use it as a main site anymore.

Some networking sites also make it easier than others to send regular announcements. Know about the places where you post your profile, and remember that while your company's image may be laid-back and friendly, a professional image is still important. Your announcements may reach beyond where you post them, and more power to them if they do. But your original postings should always be in places that support your professional image.

Internal Announcements

Your team is the lifeblood of your company. Team members want to be informed and to receive information directly, not by rumor. Selecting the right time, medium, and tone for significant internal announcements can strengthen or weaken a team. Information about personnel changes or policy decisions is better received when given directly and honestly by management before rumors and distortions heighten an already tense situation. Unfortunately, sometimes what is or is not a "perfect phrase" may have to be determined by legal counsel. Find out what you can say and how you can say it to give the most honest, up-front information you can. Do your best to announce anything that affects employees. They deserve the best information you can possibly give them.

Your company can set up numerous forms of online connections and ways to keep the team posted and in touch. Be careful not to use one medium for everything without considering the circumstances. While you may establish a pattern of posting company announcements in one place, some messages to certain departments or individuals will require more private, direct communication and will not be appropriate or appreciated if posted publicly. Although it may seem that you could save yourself a few minutes by hitting one public post, don't forget that taking the time to send a direct e-mail about a sensitive issue will make an immeasurable difference in how the message is received and in an employee's feelings about the company. Remember also that some information is still best delivered by phone or in person.

External Announcements

No matter how great your business is, how unique your products or service, no one will know unless you tell them. The smaller your company, the more likely people will have to hear the news from you. Make getting announcements out to the public a part of your weekly or monthly plan. Tout your good news, new products and services, new product reviews, company changes, awards, events, and more. If a change or event says something good about you, announce it to the world. Announcements are as good as advertisements. You just need people to see and hear your name; it doesn't have to be in a glossy, expensive ad. As a matter of fact, a press release can be more effective than an ad because it appears as an article *about* you. The more your company's name is seen or heard, the more likely it is that yours will be the name that will be recalled when someone needs your product or service.

Whether you make your announcements through press releases, newsletters, Internet updates, or other media choices, knowing when and how and how much to announce is a fine line. This world is suffering from information overload. In response, some of us tend to announce less rather than more. We don't want to be part of the problem, and we hold on to old-fashioned notions of customer, employee, and company loyalty. However, with so much information coming at people every day, if you do not communicate regularly, they may even forget about your company or simply think of the one they heard about most recently when they might have thought of you.

We tend to think that if we provide a good product or service and make customers happy, they'll tell two friends, and so on, and our business will increase exponentially. While happy customers often pass on the word, to help the process you have to at least remind them you exist. Satisfied customers are much more likely to forward your e-mailed announcement than to think of your business over dinner with friends. In the information age, subtlety is lost, and those who are too subtle will be forgotten. Announce yourself to be remembered, announce your good news, *and* be proactive about addressing bad news.

Good news travels fast. Bad news travels faster. If you have a sensitive announcement to make to the public, don't delay. You want your company's news to reach the public when, where, and how you choose before people are reading or circulating it online. With the rapid-fire spread of information and the constant blurring of public and private information and social and business networking, the line between internal and external communication is sometimes fuzzy. You know your employees should be given certain information; but they shouldn't necessarily blog or post about it. Consequently, information control becomes a sensitive and key issue. Internal controls and precise wording are critical to releasing important information about your company.

Promotional Writing Basics

Promotional writing, like all writing, should be clear, concise, and correct. Beyond that, promotional writing must attract, entice, and convince the reader or listener to visit your website, come to your place of business, or pick up the phone to take action or learn more about your company, services, or products.

Promotional writing includes, but is far beyond, the standard press release or advertisement. Any announcement you make promotes your business in some way. Even if the promotion is subtle, if it's getting your name out, it's promotional. While this book focuses on information specific to press releases and promotional writing, keep in mind that any advice about promotional writing you see or hear in books, blogs, and podcasts can provide additional valuable insights about how to phrase and where to post your company news.

E-Mail Basics

The ease of sending e-mail often leads to oversending, which is not always in your best interest. Don't oversend. That means don't send an e-mail announcement to everyone who may have once sent you an e-mail; it also means don't overburden those who are willingly on your e-mail list because they want relevant information. Oversending e-mails is the surest way to be ignored or find your way to the junk mail file. Don't let your announcements sound like white noise. E-mails should not be overused for announcements, and they should always be appropriately directed, have a clearly stated subject line, and be clear and succinct. E-mails are quick and easy to send, but that doesn't mean that they should be sent quickly and without consideration; your e-mails are as much a part of your image as any other written communication.

Your subject line is critical to catching your audience's attention. A reader not taken with a newspaper headline might still glance at the article, but a reader turned off by an e-mail subject line would just as soon delete the message as open it. Use your subject as your hook. Avoid spam-alert words such as *guaranteed*, *promise*, and *get rich*. Use your e-mail signature to give websites, blogs, full contact information, or taglines. You can also use it as a way to send a brief, current phrase announcing recent good news such as "Winner of the Downtown Association's 2010 Local Business of the Year Award" or "Celebrating 15 Years of Artful Living Expos."

Blogging, Facebooking, Twittering . . .

Blogging is great for business; however, if you're making important or regular announcements on your blog, don't assume that everyone is checking in daily, weekly, or even monthly. Blogging regularly is a good way to keep your website current and let interested people know what's new, but not everyone you would want to reach will be a subscriber, and not every subscriber will check in when there's an update. If you make announcements on your blog, make that a place to go for more information, but announce your news more prominently as well. At the very least, be sure to note new announcements on your website's home page.

Better still, turn people's attention toward your business by making your announcement in an e-mail or newsletter or any print or online media that's likely to drive people *to* your website or into your store where they'll find more information.

If you have news that you want to get right out and you want it to stand out, send out an "Update" to your newsletter list that will make that announcement stand apart.

If you're linked into the latest social networking media, that's the best way to make quick, immediate announcements. As we write this book, people check in regularly to Facebook and Twitter, and who knows what will be next? Watch and wait before you put your time and energy into posting announcements on a social media site that might not take off, but if you didn't know Twitter was coming into the media fold in a big way before the 2008 elections, you knew it when Barack Obama used it to announce major campaign news and updates and when CNN starting reading "tweets" on the air. Such sites have become a part of the culture and are used by CEOs and PR companies everywhere to make regular announcements.

These sites offer an opportunity to connect with employees and customers in a new way, promote yourself, learn what people are saying, see what your competitors are announcing, and take word-of-mouth advertising to new levels. Twitter, for instance, lets you post a question for immediate response to obtain feedback or a quick market test of ideas—and good ideas will spread quickly. Such a posting can serve as a combination focus group, press release, and way to show your company's personality.

Words Are Forever

The right phrase can be memorable, inspiring, or motivating, while a flip or badly worded phrase can cause confusion, misunderstandings, and negative feelings. On the other hand, a slip of the pen (or keyboard) can not only spread through the company rumor mill in a flash, it can become international news within seconds. These days, anything you put into print or on video can be transmitted around the world in an instant.

Think of any phrase you put out into the world in connection with your company as permanent. A tweet, for example, seems fleeting, but everything you post is stored. Once in cyberspace, a message may be impossible to remove, and bad information spreads as quickly as—actually, more quickly than—good information. Consequently, you have to think more carefully than ever before about your messages, your language, and even the unanticipated inferences that others may draw from what you write.

What Works for You?

While instant information has exciting advantages, always keep in mind the potential downsides as well. Craft all of your communications with clarity and purpose and be certain that the statements they make are understandable, positive, and impactful. Keeping that in mind, new and expanding ways to communicate can be used to great advantage, allowing you to make company announcements more regularly and in more venues than ever before. Try things, track effectiveness the best you can, ask clients how they found you, and ask others what they're doing that's working. As you explore, continue to use announcement venues that are tried and true—and always try to be true to your own style.

Chapter 2

Style

"Style is primarily a matter of instinct."

—Bill Blass

What's your style? You should have a style that announces who you are, but sometimes in considering your audience or media, you may change your style somewhat. Overall, though, know who you are. Know yourself and your company and be who you are. That will make your announcements more memorable. As you take phrases from this book or construct your own, alter them as needed to fit your style. You might need to tailor a phrase—shorten it, add a few frills, or even stitch two together—to make it fit just right. It's your image, your appearance. Suit yourself with the perfect phrase and wear it well!

Target Your Audience

Some businesses target specific audiences exclusively; many target different audiences for varying products and services, whether based on age, gender, income level, or any one of thousands of identifiers such as single mothers, hikers, dog lovers, etc. Whoever your audience, target your message. For instance, if you're speaking mainly to high-level executives, you'll use different language than you would use in targeting college students. As you construct your messages, consider your audience. If you can use different voices and announcements to target different markets, you'll be more likely to capture attention within each group. More than ever, you can now send multiple announcements at little or no cost, so even mass marketing can be more targeted than ever before.

Know your market and, as always, remember to align the medium and the message to it. As you know, different audiences respond to different media. Some will get most of their information from print material such as newspapers, magazines, or mailers. Others will only read what is on their computer screen. Are you selling to people who have just about given up reading print material? To target college kids on Twitter, use Twitter language and reference points that interest them. You can send announcements about the same product through a mailing directed to seniors, but use language and examples that will speak to them and their needs, hopes, and dreams. Your task is not only to choose the message and language for your audience but also to select the medium that is most likely to get your audience's attention.

Pinpoint Your Message

How can you make your announcement stand out? What's the most important point in your message? If your announcement is about a new product, don't emphasize that several other products are great, too. Focus on one strong, clear message.

Keep it concise and to the point. You can always follow up or route people to more information about other products, but don't overwhelm your audience. If the product is added to a particular line, of course that's part of the message, but focus on where you want to draw your customers' attention.

The same is true for internal announcements. We've all received e-mail that's so long we save it for later and may or may not get back to it. It may seem that the more content you send the more informative your announcement is, but the opposite is usually true. Information overload is likely to cause reader shutdown. Keep e-mail announcements brief and to the point, and make the most important information stand out.

If you have a critical message to share, don't add a "by the way" item. Focus on the change in health benefits, the holiday party, or the team-building workshop. State your purpose succinctly and follow with clear, concise points. If you have several topics on the same announcement, make sure to separate sections with clear, bold, descriptive headlines that make the message easy to scan or reference and, most important, will readily draw the eye to areas of the greatest interest or priority.

Get the Phrase Out!

If you have an announcement to make that deserves special attention, repeat it and send it in more than one way. For instance, if it's an internal announcement, highlight it in the monthly newsletter and send out a special announcement as well. If you're in a physical office environment, you can also post it on a wall; in a cyber office, post it where everyone will see it when checking in. A public announcement can be blasted out in a number of ways and should be sent through a number of channels. Though it may be best to target some external announcements to specific audiences, most should be shouted out as far and wide as you can.

When reaching out to clients and customers, you have more avenues available than ever before. Choose them and use them wisely. Beyond advertising and your own website, newsletter, or blog, as you explore new ways to reach out, continue to always be aware of your image. If the free service that offers to promote your business announcements is filled with pop-up ads and spams your prospects, that "free service" will be very costly to your business.

There are, however, many respectable free and low-cost ways to reach out that will enhance your image and visibility. Paid services should also be considered and budgeted for when appropriate to get your announcements out. As you construct your perfect phrases, they'll go farther and reach new audiences if you think creatively about ways to reach out and be noticed.

Image Matters

Whether your announcement or invitation travels with a postage stamp or a mouse click, remember that any announcement you generate makes a statement about your company and, in a small business, you. Just as you pay attention to your appearance for a face-to-face meeting—even organize your desk a bit for that meeting in your office—your written material shouts "This is who I am!" Is your announcement simple, catchy, clear, and concise? Is your tone professional, inviting, and friendly?

Whatever medium you choose, make your announcement stand out. Take advantage, if you can, of white space, complementary colors, and eye-catching icons. If your announcement is text only and more than a single line or two, make your message stand out by keeping the text blocks brief, putting the most important information first, and closing with a punch. Even the most brilliant phrase will be ineffective if no one notices it. If you're dealing with elements beyond text, such as formatting choices, did you select a font that was higher on readability or personality? Did you choose colors for contrast or subtlety?

What's Your Style?

As you communicate regularly with staff and clients, your written style will emerge. Think about your overall style and how you choose to come across: authoritative, professional, caring, folksy, efficient (to name a few possibilities). The pace of a message is part of your style, too. Do you use short, punchy words and short sentences? Or even just fragments? Do you use more of a longhand, elegant approach? In some cases, your style will come naturally in the way that best reflects you and the image you wish to project. For an example of the wide variety of styles you can use, compare the following announcements: "Art show with snacks, music, and more!" and "We invite you to join us for an art exhibition featuring hors d'oeuvres and classical guitar." Whichever style you choose, try to create a consistent personality for your company.

Part Two

The Perfect Phrase

In this section, you will find some perfect phrases that are perfect for you and some that you can modify to suit your style and your particular situation. You may also find your imagination sparked with new phrases. We suggest not only tabbing pages and making notes of useful phrases you find here but also creating your own store of phrases as they come to you. In Part Three, we will offer suggestions for brainstorming, creating, and polishing your own perfectly unique phrases that speak directly to your audience. But first, here in Part Two, "The Perfect Phrase," you will find perfect phrases for a wide range of announcements as well as the mindsets behind developing announcements for each topic.

Chapter 3

Company News

"I went to a restaurant that serves 'breakfast any time,' so I ordered French toast during the Renaissance."
—Steven Wright

Company news will have a different focus depending on whether it is announced to employees, investors, subscribers, or the world. The main focus of this chapter is on news to be announced outside of the company. (Chapters 6 and 7 concentrate exclusively on announcements to your team.) As always, write to your audience—*and write regularly.*

Place a high priority on keeping your company name and news in the minds of clients, subscribers, buyers, and the world (or at least whichever segments of the world are most interested in your product, service, or cause). Think about not only what, when, and how to announce but also where. Consider varied outlets, and always be willing to investigate new options. Some announcement venues will be free, and others should be factored into the budget. If you're running a small company, make sure that someone is assigned to PR or hire an outside PR person. Don't miss opportunities to get your company news out!

Newsletters

Perfect Announcement Mindsets

- By offering an online newsletter monthly or quarterly, you can reach a huge market for a relatively small cost. Newsletters are a wonderful vehicle for sharing information with clients and customers.

- Many companies have either supplemented or replaced hard copy paper newsletters with an online version, which can make the occasional printed piece a nice change of pace.

- Offer something to generate interest in reading the newsletter. Specials entice, and sharing free advice and information engages existing and prospective customers by showing them what you know and that you have a genuine interest in sharing useful information with them.

- Give your newsletter some style. If it's informative without being eye-catching, few people will read far enough to find your great content.

- Be creative in content. Elicit ideas from employees.

- Newsletter columns give employees an opportunity to share knowledge and expertise.

- Consider whether monthly themes work for you. Before you decide, think of at least twenty-four themes that relate to what you do.

- Employee spotlights, such as "Employee of the Month," make people feel appreciated and proud of the jobs they are doing. As long as the recipients are chosen fairly, these columns can also engender a sense of camaraderie.

- Anytime you receive publicity elsewhere or have a press release published, refer to it in your newsletter.

- Have some fun with your newsletter. You can be informative and still make people smile.

- If you're sending an online newsletter, most programs will provide an unsubscribe line and built-in unsubscribe feature. If you're sending direct via e-mail, be sure to include a way for recipients to unsubscribe. It's simple Internet etiquette to make it easy for people to unsubscribe and to say how long the action typically takes before it goes into effect.

Phrases

- "Have You Seen Us in *The Street*? If you haven't seen the article about our new initiatives in the *Wall Street Journal*, visit the Press Page on our website!"

- "This Month's Theme: A Helping Hand"

- "Quote of the Month: 'No one is useless in the world who lightens the burdens of another.'—Charles Dickens"

- "Click here to download our monthly podcast!"

- "Our Online Entrepreneur of the Month: Lynn Nelson. Click here to read the full interview and see what Lynn says is her number one reason for success!"

- "Have you seen our website lately? Click our logo to visit and see all-new sections, new articles, and an introduction to our newest writers."

- "Each month we put the spotlight on our star employee. This month's star is Bruce Wayland."
- "Send your feedback and questions for our 'Client Chat' column. We look forward to hearing from you!"
- "Bring this newsletter for a 15% discount. Thank you for subscribing!"
- "Please take our reader survey. All responses will be confidential, and your comments will be carefully considered. Thank you for taking the time to help us serve you better."
- "If you have any comments about the *Campers' Digest* newsletter, please write to comments@cdn.org. Thank you!"
- "We hope that this message has been valuable. However, if you wish to unsubscribe, click here. You will be removed from the list within the next week. Thank you for your interest over the term of your subscription. We hope you will visit our website again."
- "Share with friends! If you find this newsletter valuable, tell your friends and colleagues about it. If three people sign up and fill in your name in the 'referred by' box, we'll send you a special thank-you gift!"

Press Releases

Perfect Announcement Mindsets

- A press release must have some news value to be picked up. Great press release topics include awards, events, promotions, new products and services, and new initiatives that respond to current news and trends.

- Press releases must be timely, accurate, and informative, but they can also be fun.

- While the standard press release still reaches numerous media outlets, potential reach and available options have increased exponentially; choose your distribution service wisely.

- Headings should be brief and eye-catching. (For tips on writing great headings, see Chapter 12.) Articles should answer the basic reporter questions: Who? What? When? Where? Why?

- The "About" section should be a brief, boilerplate statement that provides company background.

- Don't be timid or modest. When you are the company president and chief cook and bottle washer, it's usually beneficial to remain visible in the public eye. People like to see the face behind a company.

- Remember to publicize every talk, every charitable event, and every activity for a business or community organization—everything and anything that could be considered news.

- Don't forget to send your press release to trade magazines, journals, newsletters, and alumni publications.

- Stories should be in third person, as if written by a reporter. Even if you write your own press release and are writing about yourself (as the company president, for example), write articles, press releases, or news in the third person.

- Include quotes. Quotes from you, employees, clients, or others involved in the story personalize your content. Quotes by people in the news or commenting on current events that relate to your story anchor your news in the present and make your story feel more current so recipients are likely to read and forward it more immediately. Famous quotes that relate to your story can add an element of interest and may increase your odds of being found in a search or forwarded by someone who loves the quote and how your story illustrates it.

- Use short paragraphs. Short paragraphs and sentences facilitate a fast read. Your final paragraph should be short, giving clear information or direction on what you wish the reader to do next.

- Consider when the intended audience will be reading your piece and use the correct tense.

- Avoid using jargon, slang, acronyms, or industry terms unless your message is strictly targeted only to those who are familiar with these terms. Yes, a lot of catchy jargon and acronyms work but only for the right audience. Readers have to know what you mean.

- Another value to the press release is that an editor may decide that your news is worth a feature article.

Phrases

- "Please join us for our Grand Opening event on Saturday, November 1, from noon until 4:00 P.M. as we open our new environmental center with a ribbon cutting by the mayor. Enjoy fun, educational games for the kids and a first look at our unique, hands-on exhibits. The special Grand Opening events continue all weekend with music in the Courtyard on Saturday evening at 7:00 P.M. and a free behind-the-scenes tour on Sunday morning at 10:00 A.M."

- "Minda Williams, president of Gifts Now, will be the keynote speaker at the annual National Promotional Items Conference in Baton Rouge, Louisiana."

- "Mika Spielberg, president of Line It Up, will address the Somerset Chamber of Commerce on Tuesday, July 17, at 7:00 P.M. about online marketing techniques."

- "The Ocean County Library received a donation of online learning tools from Anderson Software. Cary Anderson, president and CEO, will give a demonstration of the new programs at an Open House on Thursday, March 19, at 2:00 P.M. Assisting Anderson in this demonstration will be two Orange High students, Matthew Berkin and Tamara Fisher."

- "Phyllis More, founder of More Furnishings, has created More for Children, a coordinating arm for all local efforts to bring school supplies, games, and books to local disadvantaged youth."

- "The Madison Chamber of Commerce recently honored Thomas King, founder and president of Action

Realty, as businessperson of the year. King's other honors include a Senate citation for assisting young entrepreneurs and an award for his recent book, *Every House Is Someone's Dream*."

- "Dr. Melissa Ivers, chief of staff at MBM Hospital since 1990, has been selected to serve on the Governor's Council for Diagnostic Research."

- "Leo Barr, local children's book author, will spend Friday at the Wilson Elementary School, reading to students in the lower grades and coaching fourth and fifth graders in writing stories. He will not, however, be autographing books, saying that children don't want his autograph, but he takes it as a great compliment: 'Kids become very upset when some weird guy—let alone anyone—writes in their favorite books!'"

- "Extra! Extra! *Our Town News* is now online at www.our townnews.com. We will continue to bring you the news in print, as you've been enjoying it, and now our online site offers more photos, a new online-only "About Town" column, and special features including archives, opinion polls, and an expanded local calendar of events guide that will be updated every Thursday morning. Our new site covers virtually everything you'd want to know about Our Town News!"

- "Veggie Sprouts restaurant announces the winner of its Meatless Meatball Recipe Competition: Scarlett Kincaid of Crawford, Indiana, created the most delectable meatless meatballs for the Veggie Sprouts competition. Scarlett's reward will be a complimentary dinner for six at Veggie Sprouts, an individual membership in the

Humane Society of the United States, and a new menu item in her name: 'Scarlett's Meatless Meatballs.'"

- "Emma Mason, class of '85, has been named senior counsel to the president of Mega Foods, Inc."

- "Ron Edgar Dupree, class of 2006, is the recipient of the Chicago Art Museum's Up and Coming Artist award."

- "Rhonda Sage, president of the class of '04, is the recipient of the University's Graduate Author Award."

New Customer Service Initiatives

Perfect Announcement Mindsets

- Maintain existing customers by building on customer loyalty and satisfaction.

- Satisfied customers can expand your base; they are walking advertisements.

- Remember that although customer satisfaction is often hard to measure in concrete terms of return on investment, it should never be undervalued.

- Be clear about what you can afford to offer and what you can't afford not to offer.

- Be savvy in creating new customer service initiatives. Understand changing markets and monitor competitor initiatives. Learn what it takes to stand out. Develop your own brand; make your look and style as distinctive as possible.

- Study customer needs through customer advisory boards, focus groups, feedback sessions, and/or questionnaires.

- Remember your regular base when creating promotions to attract new customers.

- Focus on customer needs and wants.

- Finding ways to offer something for nothing will bring traffic, word-of-mouth referrals, goodwill, and customers who not only feel they're getting additional value but feel valued by you.

Phrases

- "We're celebrating 35 years in business! To thank our loyal customers, we're offering a special anniversary sale with additional discounts for anyone who uses our store charge card during September."

- "How is our service? Complete our service evaluation and receive a 15% discount on your next purchase."

- "We know our customers are watching their change, so we're changing our annual sale to offer deeper discounts on more great merchandise!"

- "Tough times call for caring service providers. Our prices show how priceless you are to us."

- "You asked, we listened. Visit us online to see our new products, features, and tutorials. You'll like what you see!"

- "Difficult times shouldn't mean impossible choices. You don't have to choose between low prices and high quality. We believe that you should have it all!"

- "Green is in. At MIRA, it was never out."

- "Indulge your taste without betraying your conscience. Earth Friendly Goodies, a unique outlet shop, buys only from environmentally and socially responsible companies. Shop without worry at www.earthfriendlygoodies.com."

- "To better serve our core market, Acropolis is including customer representatives on its new advisory board."

- "Because you have been a valued client for the past decade, we would welcome your participation on our newly formed Customer Advisory Board."

Perfect Announcement Mindsets

■ Focus on features and benefits.

■ Offer introductory rates. If you can announce a special offer for buying newly released products, such as introductory rates or other special deals, your product launch will have more fuel for liftoff.

■ Use descriptive words that paint a picture and evoke emotion.

■ Use words that inspire people to imagine themselves enjoying the benefits of your products.

■ Announce in venues that reach both existing and new customers.

■ Reach out to all potential demographic markets. Viable media and outlets vary among age groups and cultures.

■ When announcing product launch events, remember to focus on your readers' needs and desires. Make the event sound enticing and stress the benefits such as the opportunity for a sneak preview of new products or launch party discounts.

■ Announce launch events far in advance and post or send reminders.

Phrases

■ "Treat your tired feet to our plush new Cozywear slippers! For total full-body luxury, slide them on and then wrap yourself in our velvety soft Cozywear robe."

- "If you love our voice recording application, you'll love creating e-cards with our new Truevoice e-card application! A good card will speak to someone's heart—a great card will do it in the sender's own voice!"

- "This month only, buy one design product and receive another at half price."

- "Our new technology will change the way you do business. Come to our launch celebration and try it out. You won't want to leave without it."

- "We know that you loved our high-end electronic models. Now try the same quality in our stimulus models."

- "Come see what's new!"

- "You asked, we answered! Our new product line was developed in response to customer comments and suggestions. Thank you for sharing your thoughts with us and helping us grow in new directions!"

- "If you loved the ease of our products before, you'll be amazed by how much more user friendly they are now!"

- "We've expanded our menu! Jacques Bistro now offers new menu items but don't worry—we still have your favorites!"

- "Come see the new menu at The Pita Pocket, where our overstuffed pockets exceed your expectations, and prices leave lots of lettuce in your pockets!"

- "*Please touch!* How else will you know how much fun our new products are to use?"

- "Sign up for our services at the launch party and receive a 15% discount on any one of our special packages!"

New Services

Perfect Announcement Mindsets

- Explain improvements.

- Announce new services in venues that reach both existing and new customers.

- Announce directly to existing customers through mail or e-mail.

- Let clients know that you appreciate their business and are actively working to find ways to serve them better.

- Keep up-to-speed with advances in customer services so that your customers have all the latest advantages.

- If you see a service in a different industry that's not common in yours, think about whether you can adapt it for your customers.

- Put a value-added component into an existing service.

- Expand a service in a way that gives the customer something more but doesn't cost you more.

- Expand an existing service to keep pace with changing times.

- Partner with a complementary business to build on a service.

Phrases

- "Our outstanding service just got even better! We have now have online appointment scheduling, online chat support, and a new feedback forum. Our goal is to serve you better."

- "We now offer access to all of your customer records online."

- "No more long lines! We're now online so that you can shop any time. No lines, no waiting, and our customer service team is available online and at 1-800-055-0001."

- "What makes The Newcomer different from the competition? Visit our newest location and see for yourself."

- "New gift card policy! Gift cards will no longer expire. Any gift card purchased for you can be redeemed any time, any day, any year. We appreciate that you and your friends and loved ones care enough to give the gift of choosing something special from our store. The card is a gift, and a gift should never expire."

- "We now offer automated appointment reminders to your phone and/or e-mail. With busy schedules, it's easy to forget appointments, and your ongoing care is important. Our 24-hour cancellation policy is a necessity for us, but we want to make it easy and stress-free for you. Relax! Our goal is to take good care of you."

- "As an added service to accommodate our clients, you may send your questions to query@sandler.com. We'll respond within 24 hours. If your query is urgent, please put 'urgent' in the subject line."

- "We now have more phone support than ever, and your calls will be answered only by qualified professionals who understand your concerns and are trained to offer you premium service. We're making changes to serve you better. Call any time!"

- "DA invites you to the first training preview for our clients. Three of our top training consultants will present an overview and a 10-minute demo of a new or newly refined program."

- "Keep your skin looking young and feeling fresh! Not Just Hair has added an onsite cosmetologist to our expanding array of beauty professionals."

- "Your clothes are an essential part of your image. Now, in addition to unbeatable cleaning, Mercedes Cleaners will help you 'sew' the seeds for your success with quality alterations at a fair price. We've just hired Maria Campo, a first-rate tailor, to give your clothing a custom fit."

- "We'll pick up your clothes, take them for a spin, and have them back to your door in 24 hours! In response to our customers' requests, we've added free pickup and delivery to our laundry service."

- "The Shopper, your local concierge, just added five venues to our list of restaurants and retailers. If your favorite places don't offer delivery services, check again. Visit www.theshopperservice.com to find out who's partnered with us to serve you better!"

Perfect Announcement Mindsets

- In annual and quarterly reports, accountants express an opinion to the best of their knowledge that a company's finances are as shown and are shown in comparison to the previous year. These must follow strict guidelines.

- Investors want information, and they will need updates and announcements in between reports, especially in response to news that impacts or relates to the company.

- Investors want assurances.

- Keep your language clear and simple.

- Other than annual or quarterly reports or newsletters, focus on one item per communication.

- Share troubling news that will be public anyway. Say what you are doing to protect shareholders.

- Be accurate. Investors lose faith when companies have to announce a restatement of financial earnings.

- Notify investors of changes within the company's structure and/or management.

- Share good news; it boosts confidence.

- Privately held companies, those with fewer than 35 shareholders, may have fewer formal announcements than publicly held companies.

Phrases

- "Fourth-quarter earnings reflect the impact of cutting costs without minimizing quality."

- "Thank you for your ongoing confidence and support; we will continue to earn it."
- "New product launch boosts earnings."
- "The current economic climate has led our Board of Directors to make the following changes to protect your assets: . . ."
- "The recent downturn is beginning to turn upward again, and PHM Corp. is at the forefront of this move."
- "Recent management changes created an even stronger leadership team."
- "Our streamlined product line has produced a stronger quarter than anticipated."
- "Maggie O'Shea, senior investment advisor, is the recipient of the *Investors' Quarterly* Top Ten Award."
- "BCD Announces Second Quarter Earnings: BCD Inc. announced today that net income for the quarter ended on June 30, 2010, was $3.6 million, or $0.28 per diluted share for the quarter ended June 30, 2010."
- "BUF, Ltd., will announce financial results for the second quarter of 2010 following the market close on Wednesday, July 21, 2010. Management will conduct a video conference call to discuss the results of the last quarter and the company's outlook for the third quarter. Investors should call the company or visit the website to learn about how to dial into the call, which will take place at 10:00 A.M. EST on Wednesday, August 4, 2010."
- "ABC is pleased to announce a new alliance with Sesame Corp. For details, please visit our website."

- "Digitrack Corp. announces new management. Geoffrey Stanton, Vice President, Global Finance, is leaving Digitrack and will be replaced by Ravit Marom, who served for the past nine years as CFO of Net Grid, Ltd., and has a master's in business administration from MIT. Marom will assume the VP role on October 15, 2011."
- "EWE has, once again, beaten projected earnings. Click on our latest press release to see what the analysts are saying!"

Chapter 4

Customer Care and Events

"We see our customers as invited guests to a party, and we are the hosts. It's our job every day to make every important aspect of the customer experience a little bit better."

—Jeff Bezos

Your customers are your most valuable asset. Treat them well, acknowledge their value to your business, and reinforce their importance. Remember, the customer watches your ledger because it affects your pricing and his or her wallet. When planning, remember that the smallest gesture sometimes reaps the largest gratitude. In fact, some people may be less impressed by an extremely lavish event when the economy is tough. A customer who thinks your prices are high will always appreciate service enhancements but might question the value behind your prices if the money seems to be going into such expenses as high-end events.

New Online Features

Perfect Announcement Mindsets

- The more online features you have, the more chances you have to hold interest, provide great service, and make visiting your site easy, fun, and beneficial.

- It's hard to have the competitive edge without a comprehensive, user-friendly website.

- If you now offer ways to apply or submit information online, stress the convenience when you announce it.

- Anything you do to personalize the online experience is big news to potential users of your site, who have become accustomed to greater and greater levels of customization on many of the websites they use regularly.

- If you add a new feature that could conceivably replace an old feature, make a point of saying either that it will be a replacement or that the old, familiar feature will still remain on the site in addition to the new one.

- Most people are environmentally conscious and appreciate the green appeal of going paperless.

- Some great online features that will excite existing and potential customers include online applications, account information, searchable databases, new video or audio download or upload capability—anything that makes your site more user-friendly or adds convenience or fun to the overall experience of going to your website.

Phrases

- "Now you can apply online! Send your application with the click of a button, and you'll have our response within one week."

- "Our website is now easier to search, navigate, and personalize to your needs. We're working harder to make your day easier!"

- "We now offer customer reviews to help you search for a brand you love from a seller you can trust."

- "We now offer customized e-alerts! Choose the topics that interest you most and let us know whether you'd like to receive alerts of new articles and posts every day, week, or month. We'll keep you from missing important articles and save you time by letting you know, at your convenience, when we've posted something you won't want to miss!"

- "Personal shopping alerts! Tell us what you're looking for, and we'll e-mail you when it comes in. We can even notify you by text message."

- "Let's save a forest! We now offer online statements and a full account history online. Call or sign up online to go paperless today!"

- "If a picture is worth a thousand words, a video tells it all! Come see the new 'Videos' tab on our website to find demonstrations, tutorials, and more."

- "Now you can upload videos to our site!"

- "Visit our new online conference center. New features and real-time streaming bring the conference to you.

Recorded archives ensure that you can see all of your favorite speakers and not miss a thing!"

- "Now you can find things even more easily with our new search feature and fully linked index page."

- "Our weekly commentary will now be recorded and available as a free podcast. Subscribe today!"

- "We now have an RSS feed so that you can receive abstracts, articles, and updates on your desktop or browser."

- "Our calendar of events now features a complete searchable database."

- "Express yourself at www.webezforyou.com! Our new web features allow you to create a fully customized page with your favorite themes, colors, and widgets. It's easier than ever to add photos, choose colors, and create a page that represents who you are and what you do."

- "We now offer tech support through video conferencing! Text and phone support will still be available, but now you'll have a 'face-to-face' option."

- "Now you can create your own profile on Heart of Nature Porthole! Find groups, network, create surveys, and make great new connections with a common interest in the environment."

- "Our new website makes it easy to search for groups you might be interested in and organize new groups by interest or geographic region. We're bringing people together!"

- "Do you tweet? We're now on Twitter. Join us there!"

- "Now on Twitter, Facebook, and LinkedIn. Let's stay connected!"

Perfect Announcement Mindsets

■ Focus on customer wants and needs.

■ Think about win/win offers to keep customers satisfied and your business in the black.

■ Think about announcing an ongoing sale corner for a store or sale items for businesses and services.

■ Though people always look to save money, tough economic times reinforce the value of discounts and sales to market to and attract new customers and build customer loyalty.

■ If you are selling major items such as cars, allow customers the option of leaving and returning within a short, defined time period for the same offer. "Now or never" is not appealing for many and makes customers wonder whether you don't have the confidence to allow them to sleep on it or do a little research.

■ If your company is in an industry known for high pressure and you want to stand out and make people comfortable, announce a pressure-free sale experience. People need to weigh choices, especially during difficult times.

■ Developing a block or neighborhood sale consortium for creative marketing options can increase your advertising and clientele and also connect you with others who can come up with and implement ideas that you might not have on your own.

■ Announce special discounts for those who bring in new customers.

Phrases

- "Relax, beautify . . . and save money, too! Buy one spa service and receive a second one at 25% off."

- "Money tight? Don't sweat it! We're extending our July blowout sale to last all summer long!"

- "Attend an XYZ Spring Seminar and receive a free follow-up telephone or e-mail consultation for up to six months following the seminar."

- "Refer a client and receive 15% off any service!"

- "Drinks are on us every Tuesday this summer! Come for dinner and receive one free drink per person every Tuesday night through August."

- "Our spring specials will make your smile bloom!"

- "Our Fall Frenzy sale is blowing through this weekend only! Breeze in to find savings of up to 70% on the premium brands you love. Seasons change; quality is forever!"

- "Deep discount days continue through May 15!"

- "Stimulus sale! Invest in yourself without breaking the bank."

- "Community stimulus plan: 25% off for [town] residents during our 20% off sale."

- "Pick up your Resident Discount Card. Always 5% off; additional discounts on sale merchandise."

- "Zero coupon day: Buy our newest skin care product and get 20% off two additional items."

- "Bonus buys! Buy two clothing items and receive a third for half price."

- "One big banking family: Fedco offers $50 for every new customer referred who opens an account at any of our branches or online."

- "Now through August you can save 40% on our monthly rates. Click here to find out how!"

- "Special Sales on Back-to-School Must-Haves!"

- "To honor fathers / mothers / grandparents, we're lowering prices for Father's Day / Mother's Day / Grandparents' Day!"

- "Did you know that Administrative Assistants' Day is coming up? Show your gratitude! Browse our large selection of cards and special tokens of appreciation."

- "Free vase / card / carnation with every gift purchase! (Offer good while supplies last.)"

- "Check back with www.MusicLovers.com every week for a different weekly special! Or you can follow musiclovers on Twitter and get a weekly tweet with the special."

Contests

Perfect Announcement Mindsets

- Once you announce a contest, many will enter and become fully invested; others will be intrigued to watch events unfold. Either way, you have their attention.

- Inviting customers to participate in decisions that affect the products they buy strengthens their brand loyalty.

- Create contests to engage customers and clients. Announcing a contest pulls people together—and toward your business.

- Some contests can help you find creative people to revive or strengthen your image. If you're looking for a new logo, a "design a logo" contest spreads the job out to lots of creative minds and can yield a fantastic design for the cost of running your contest. The designer benefits from the exposure and whatever prize you choose to offer.

- Think of all the ways you might involve customers or clients in assisting you in product or service design and in marketing.

- A contest can be a way to advertise yourself, generate a buzz by offering a prize that will entice people to send the announcement of your contest to friends and colleagues, and potentially gain something that will benefit your company, such as a design, photo, tagline, or story.

- You can involve even more people by inviting votes and/or feedback on all designs submitted or just a few finalists.

- Develop an "advertise your favorite product" campaign.

- Partner with other businesses to expand the contest's reach and share the cost.

Phrases

- "Logo Contest: Our logo needs a fresh look, and we want to look good to you! Five finalists will be selected to be voted on by users at our website. We're excited to see your creativity bring new life to our look!"

- "Wanted: Outrageous ideas for new product packaging. Win and get your name on our launch materials."

- "Tell us what you like most about our product / service in 25 words or less and win a tour of our facility and a night on the town."

- "We're adding a new member to our line of Cuddle Pals. Look at the photo and submit your name suggestion. If your name is chosen, you'll receive credit on the tag and 10 of the new Cuddle Pals just in time for holiday gift-giving!"

- "Enter our nature photography contest! Winning photographs will be used to decorate products in our Beautiful World accessory line. Contest winners will receive $100 and a set of products featuring the photo. Please send up to three of your best nature photographs for consideration. To see how your photo might look on one of our products, download our sample templates. For complete guidelines, visit www.beautifulworldaccessories.com."

- "Win a set of our new dishware! Enter our 'Name That Dish' contest and if we choose your name for our new line, we'll send you a complete set."

- "Want to prepare your recipe on a famous TV cooking show? Submit your recipe and a video to production team@cookshows.com."

- "Enter to win $1,000! Everyone is belt-tightening these days. We're looking for the most innovative or the most effective methods our readers have found. Tell us what steps you're taking to keep down expenses. If you've seen a dramatic change in your finances, include that in your story. We're looking for the most helpful, inspiring, or interesting story to share in our 'Financial Fixes' column. The winner will receive story publication and a $1,000 deposit in one of our savings CDs."

- "Submit your vacation photos for a chance to win our newest digital camera!"

- "At New Sun Solutions, we bring good things to life—but that tagline is taken! Give us a great tagline that's descriptive, fun, and 10 words or fewer. If it fits us well and makes us smile, we'll award the winner with one of three exciting vacations. Please visit our website at www.newsunsolutions.com for more information."

- "The Creative Consumer Photo Contest! Have you found new, fun ways to use our products? To enter, submit photos of our products being used in creative ways. Full contest rules and guidelines are attached."

- "Don't miss the Hot Shot Photo Awards from Cool Vacation Destinations. You can compete and win in five categories: Kids at Play, Nature's Way, Animal Instincts, For the Birds, and Sights to Behold. Send your hottest shots to us by January 1 to win cool prizes. Click the camera below for complete guidelines. Go ahead. Take your best shot!"

- "They say, 'There's no such thing as a free lunch.' They're wrong. Just stop by McFees with your business card and you can win a free lunch!"

- "DunkIt Ice Cream announced its Fifth Annual "Find the Gumdrop" contest. Ten ice cream cones have gumdrops in the bottom. Those who find the gumdrops in their cones will receive store gift certificates."

- "Thanks to all who voted on the entries for our latest cartoon caption contest, and congratulations to all the winners!"

Event Announcements and Invitations

Perfect Announcement Mindsets

- Be clear about the purpose of your event.

- Type should be easy to read. The prettiest type is often the most difficult to decipher.

- Event announcements and invitations can appear in newspapers, on flyers, in e-mails, or on your website or can be mailed on stationery.

- Event announcements need a hook. Time is limited and everyone is carefully selecting where to spend not just money but time. Let people know that your event will be worth their time.

- Events can showcase products or services.

- Charity events can stir up support for your company when potential customers see that you care enough to support a good cause.

- Promote event sponsors in your literature and press releases.

- Organize an event that includes multiple businesses.

- Don't leave event highlights that might draw people in as surprises. Announce them up front, and more people will be enticed to come and enjoy the highlight, making your event a bigger success.

- Depending upon the event, the people you'd like to attract, and what you'd like to accomplish at your event, an "Invitation Only" event might be appropriate.

- Food is always a draw to an event—even if you're only offering simple hors d'oeuvres or snacks.

- Unless your event has limited space, always invite (and even entice) people to bring their friends and/or colleagues.

Phrases

- "Join us for this exciting / thought-provoking / deliciously taste-filled / unique / heartwarming / extraordinary / moving / touching / fun-filled event!"

- "Please join us for a grand opening celebration featuring great music, a sidewalk chalk art contest for the kids, face painting, and more!"

- "We're back! Please join us for our grand reopening celebration. We're better than ever with more brands, more sales, and more of what you're looking for. Bring this announcement to receive a special door prize!"

- "By invitation only, Starr Jewelers will hold a Thank-You Blast at the Seashore Club with food, drink, music, and gifts."

- "Please visit our cosmetics counter this weekend. We will have a fashion-industry makeup artist providing free makeup applications and beauty advice."

- "Present, past, and future customers are invited to our second annual Wine, Dine, and Discount shopping event."

- "Join us for our annual charity run. Let's run together for a better world!"

- "Our Summer Exchange Event: Bring a gently worn garment with the PACE label for Dress for Success and receive 25% off any new purchase."

- "Interested in our next event? Call 1-800-055-1234 or visit http://greatescapespackages/events.com for more information or to sign up for regular updates. Thank you for your interest. We look forward to seeing you at future events!"

- "Our annual Health Matters wellness event is sponsored by City Wellness Center, which has joined with us to provide health information because your health matters!"

- "Click here to view more information about this exciting event!"

- "Indigo Corp. is pleased to be the prime sponsor of the annual United Way Dinner Dance."

- "Please attend a reception and discussion about industry trends and what they mean for you!"

- "You are cordially invited to attend a showing of our 2011 automobile lineup."

- "To show our appreciation for your attendance, each guest will receive a gift certificate to one of our downtown restaurants."

- "Join us for our after-hours gallery walk! Come see the best of our city's culture as you enjoy wine and cheese and chat with gallery owners and featured artists. For more about which artists will be featured at each gallery, please visit http://ourcitygallerywalk.com. For more information, call Watercolor Dreams Gallery at 1-800-055-0000."

Conferences

Perfect Announcement Mindsets

- Your conference is competing with countless others that may interest the prospective attendees—let alone everything else they could be doing with that time and money. Your announcement has to be enticing and show the value of participating.

- Anounce your role whether you are hosting, putting on, participating in, or sponsoring the conference.

- Announce speakers and panelists when they are confirmed. If you have to announce before major speakers are confirmed, list those you have and tell where people can look to see the final list of exciting (or informative or inspiring) speakers.

- Offer enticements to bring others, especially if enrollment numbers are a concern.

- Stress what participants will learn and gain. Let them know what they'll take home—from knowledge to skills to conference giveaways.

- If your conference is in a great area, stress the location as a great place to be and to tour before or afterward.

- Use descriptive words that entice, motivate, and inspire attendance. Every conference claims to be informative. What more can you say about yours, and how can you say it? Beyond informative, will it be colorful, inventive, intriguing, or eye-opening? Say only what's true, but say it with words that intrigue!

Phrases

■ "Join us for this exciting / dramatic / electrifying / exhilarating / intriguing / lively / provocative / sensational / stimulating / energizing / informative / provocative / unique / fascinating conference!"

■ "The ABC International Literacy Expo will provide an unparalleled opportunity for networking, brainstorming, and community building with global peers in education."

■ "NRG representatives will be at the State Business Conference to explain our procurement process for small, minority, and women-owned businesses. Don't miss this information-packed presentation!"

■ "Join other professionals and practitioners for the Business of Health Marketing Expo. You can't build any business without marketing. Expand your healing reach by learning a few tricks of the marketing trade. You cannot help those who don't know how to find you. Sign up today!"

■ "This year's Astronomy Conference will be a can't-miss celebration of astronomical proportions, a program rich with varied events and activities for astronomers, professors, undergraduate students, graduate students, high school teachers, star gazers, and everyone who loves the night sky!"

■ "A panel of well-known authors will share their fascinating stories and tell how they achieved their success. All aspiring writers will be inspired and learn a few tips and tricks about the writing process and the road to publishing. For a full list of panel participants, visit our website at www.authorconferencepanel2011.com."

- "Join us for our Success Today! Conference where you will:
    - "Network with hundreds of successful people eager to share their secrets.
    - "Learn to implement our 7 Steps to Success.
    - "Establish relationships that will help you meet your goals.
    - "Attend our fabulous awards banquet.
    - "Enter to win our Success Story Award, which will be presented at the banquet.
    - "Take home knowledge, a plan for success, contacts, inspiration, and a 'Thank-You' bag filled with fantastic gifts from our event sponsors."
- "This year's Life Shots Photography Conference will feature more than 100 seminars and workshops by world-renowned experts. Our keynote speaker, Julius Milo Ramos, will discuss cutting-edge innovations in digital imaging techniques. Other presenters include world-renowned photographers and digital software developers."
- "Based on the enormous success of LMN's conferences to date, we expect this to be the largest product development seminar in the country. Nowhere else will you find such an exceptional array of speakers and organizations."
- "The 2012 Money Conference for Couples: Join experts in the fields of both relationships and finance who will teach couples how to work together on communicating about the difficult issues surrounding money and

creating practical plans for financial security. Do you argue over money? Disagree on how to spend it? Financial issues are the number one reason for divorce. It doesn't matter how much money you have; what matters is being able to communicate and plan together. We hope you'll join us!"

- "Join artists of every discipline from around the country. Special guests will discuss artistic vision and inspiration. Panels will address the current economic climate and the practical matters of making a living as an artist in the United States today. Come be inspired by artists of every style in New York City, one of the most exciting, diverse, and artistic cities in the world."

- "Join us for the Work-At-Home Entrepreneurs Conference. Share your experience and learn from others!"

- "Bring a friend for the weekend and save 15% on the total conference rate!"

- "W. Coyote of Acme Company will be participating in a panel at the Cartoon Classics Conference of Characters. For conference details, visit www.cccconference.com. We hope to see you there!"

Free Consultations

Perfect Announcement Mindsets

- Free consultations are a way to introduce your services to potential clients.

- Free consultations are an opportunity for giveback and visibility at community and business events requesting donations.

- Be specific about what you are offering and what you are not.

- Remember that what you offer for free is your showcase. Be as diligent and professional as you would be if you were getting paid.

- When offering free consultations at a company, keep them brief and try to see as many people as possible. You'll reduce your travel time and have more exposure from four 15-minute consultations than two 30-minute ones.

- Consider offering consultations in different ways. A phone or videoconferencing consultation might be enough to give potential clients a clear picture of you, but if you think your best presentation is in person, you can choose to offer other options by request and not formally announce them. If you're promoting a free consultation to bring in business, offer it in a way that allows you to make your best impression.

- Free consultations enable you to expand your contact list for future promotions and events.

Phrases

- "Meredith Consulting is donating two free 15-minute business consultations during the break at the Chamber Expo."

- "Complete the online entry and win a free 15-minute consultation during the Association Conference."

- "Complete the questionnaire attached to the registration form, and your name will be entered to win a free half-hour customer care consultation."

- "Please stop by Booth 15 at the League of Counties Conference and enter your business card to win a free one-hour computer consultation at your business."

- "We value your ongoing patronage of our salon. Please register for a free consultation in one of the categories highlighted on our website."

- "Thank you for inquiring about SAFE Financial Services. Please call to schedule a free consultation."

- "We understand that selecting a consultant is a very personal choice. We offer a free, no-obligation, introductory consultation so that you can meet us with no risk."

- "Our initial free consultation is a way for you to meet us before making a commitment. We provide a service, and you should only invest energy and resources in working with us once you know who we are and how we can serve you."

- "NewTech is offering a free equipment check to our neighbors in the Metro Building. It's our way of introducing you to our staff and services."

- "The Zone is offering free hair color consultations on Sunday from 9:00 A.M. to 3:00 P.M. If you want to make a colorful statement of self-expression, stop by to discover what color brings out your best!"

- "Get a free pass! Visit our booth at the Women Business Owner's Conference for the pass code to explore the members-only section of our website."

- "Our initial consultation is always at no charge. We want to ensure a perfect fit for you before you invest with us."

- "We gladly offer free 15-minute consultations to prospective clients."

Online Feedback Forums

Perfect Announcement Mindsets

- Feedback forums are a great way to encourage feedback to learn what's working and what isn't.

- Feedback forums should be monitored closely. You may want to approve comments before they are posted.

- You may not always be happy with feedback being shown publicly on a forum. You can invite feedback without showing it on a public forum. Consider carefully what you will do, look at other forums, and speak to people from other companies who run them.

- If you create a feedback forum, state clearly at the top of the front page what it's for and who will be checking in.

- You'll receive very negative feedback if someone posts a question expecting a response from tech support and you only have a customer service rep reviewing comments weekly. Clearly announce the purpose at the top of the forum, and make clear where people should write for immediate response or for customer support.

- Always announce forum rules and state them clearly.

Phrases

- "Check out our new Feedback Forum!"

- "This forum is designated for user suggestions and reporting."

- "This forum is for product and service comments and questions. If you're having technical issues about our website, please contact tech support. Please do not post troubleshooting questions here. We can only respond if you write directly to the department that can assist you. Write to Customer Service at cs@ourco.com or Technical Support at ts@ourco.com. We also have customer service representatives happy to help you at 1-800-001-0011."

- "Forum Rules: Please post only feedback for us and helpful suggestions for other users. No spam/advertising or offensive content. Let's keep our forum clean and friendly."

- "Please use this forum to post your feedback and make suggestions. If you are experiencing any immediate problems, please click here to write to customer service or call our service hotline at 888-001-7777. Thank you!"

- "We have one thread for posting positive transactions and one for negative. Please help us make the most of your feedback by posting in the threads provided. As we provide an interactive online community, these postings will help users evaluate those they will choose to do business with. Please be specific when posting negative feedback and realize that every user will have a chance to respond."

- "Thank you for visiting the Feedback Forum! Tell us what you think. We're listening!"

- "New at the Feedback Forum: Have you tried our new tutorials? Follow the thread to rate them and let us know what you think. We're always working to improve our products and service for your convenience!"

- "Thank you for posting!"

Product Recalls

Perfect Announcement Mindsets

■ Product recalls involve potential legal ramifications. Make sure that a lawyer familiar with your situation approves any statement. You want to do the right thing, but be sure that you don't put yourself at greater risk than necessary. Protect the public, and also protect yourself. Please note that while we offer a few basic suggestions related to writing a public recall announcement, this section does not replace the advice of any regulatory or legal expert.

■ Make the pertinent information stand out. If a recall is dangerous, say up front that the announcement is urgent.

■ All voluntary product recalls should be announced to the media and the government in order to ensure that the message reaches people who might be affected. In a formal product recall report, you will be asked to provide more detailed information, but in any announcement of a product recall you should give the most basic information as well as contact information for anyone with questions.

■ Often a company is faced with a product recall that is beyond its control. You may be the distributor and could not have known that the product was defective. You might be selling toys that are on shelves everywhere and be faced with a manufacturer's recall.

■ Sometimes, the responsibility lies with your company, and you have to bite the bullet and do what you must.

- Apologize and offer the simplest, most direct explanation.
- Do whatever you can to repair, refund, or replace the recalled product.
- Get ahead of the news by acting promptly.
- Look for and reiterate the "silver lining" of the company's appropriate response to the recall.
- Include all pertinent information and instructions in your recall announcement.

Phrases

- "We are recalling all Vibrant Brand Super X cereal because of a possible contamination, which may cause illness but is not life-threatening. We just learned that our Vibrant Brand Super X cereal may contain a contaminant from a problem in the factory city's water treatment plant. Please return the unopened or opened, used or unused box to any store that carries it. You will receive a refund and a coupon good for any two of our other products. If you have eaten any of the Vibrant Brand Super X cereal and feel at all queasy or nauseated, please see your doctor. We have been assured that these symptoms are not long-lasting or dangerous for most people, but medical treatment should be sought for your protection, comfort, and peace of mind. If you have any questions, please call our Super X Hotline at 888-010-6662. We apologize for any concern or inconvenience this announcement may cause."
- "Big Time Food Inc. is voluntarily recalling all frozen products containing cheese because we have been

advised that they may have the potential to be contaminated with *Listeria monocytogenes*. There have been no reported illnesses associated with the identified product. The product involved in the recall has the UPC number _____."

- "Urgent Shock Wave Recall of AC Power Cords. Shock Wave is instituting a nationwide recall of certain Shock Wave devices that may have defective AC power cords manufactured by WE Electrics Manufacturing Corporation. We have discovered that the power cord's prongs may crack and fail at or inside the plug. The potential risks from this power cord failure include electrical shock, device failure, and fires. These failures may lead to potential serious injury or death. Please return your product for a full refund and call 1-800-00SHOCK if you have any questions. We care for your safety and are taking prompt action to ensure the well-being of our customers."

- "Urgent Product Recall for Outdoor Playset Slides by Fun Fun Corp. We are issuing a voluntary recall and asking customers to stop using the new Fun Fun Lightning-Fast Slide immediately. We have found that some of the support structure can become loose or detached, posing a fall hazard. We have received one report of a structural element becoming detached, but no injuries have been reported. We are providing a free repair kit with replacement parts or a full replacement in some cases. For additional information, contact Fun Fun toll free at 1-800-FUN4YOU or e-mail us at customerservice@fun fun.com. We apologize for the inconvenience and are taking prompt action to ensure product safety. We care about your kids!"

Chapter 5

Announcing Transitions to the Public

"Change is inevitable—except from a vending machine."

—Robert C. Gallagher

Some transitions result from natural evolution, others from economic, customer, and employee needs. Transition may be difficult, but it's also necessary in order for a business to grow and thrive. Whatever the transition, even positive change causes ripples. Announcements should always be crafted with care. Even changes that will ultimately be positive and appreciated by most will be met with resistance. People don't always take easily to change, and sometimes people don't know what they want until they're exposed to something unknown that makes them say, "They should have done this years ago!"

Perfect Announcement Mindsets

- Renovation and expansion are usually great news. If your renovation is planned as a result of structural or other negative issues, look on the bright side—you're updating and beautifying, even if it wasn't in the plan (or the budget). You won't draw people in out of excitement (or even interest or pity) by telling them that your air conditioning system leaked and ruined your paint and carpet, but customers will be happy to hear you're making positive changes, and they may drop in to see your new look. Present information from a positive perspective.

- Relocation may be because business is good or it isn't; however, announcing the move as positive keeps the buzz positive.

- Always thank customers or clients for their business and for their patience.

- Stress all of the positive attributes of the renovation so customers will feel it's worth the wait and inconvenience.

- When expanding or relocating, if staff is remaining, say so. Customers like consistency when the product or service is good.

- Let people know when you expect to be cleaned up or up and running.

- Consider your neighbors. Will construction noise and activity affect nearby businesses? Alert them. Offer a "nice neighbor" gift of cookies or fruit.

Phrases

- "Please forgive our dust! We're renovating and beautifying to serve you better! We thank you for your business and your patience during this time."

- "Please excuse the inconvenience during our partial facelift. Renovations will be complete by March 1."

- "Metro Pub regrets the inconvenience to our customers of our temporary closing. We will reopen on July 1 with a new look and the same great food and caring service."

- "Thanks to your generous contributions, the foundation will be renovating the meeting rooms and the daycare center. We appreciate your patience during our construction. The new meeting rooms and daycare center will open with a celebration event October 11."

- "We've taken a good look at our stores and, frankly, we think they're ready for an update. We're closed for temporary upgrades as we lighten up our look. Come visit our newly, brightly, happily renewed stores when they reopen on August 1!"

- "We appreciate you, our neighbor, putting up with the inconvenience and noise our facelift is causing. Please accept this basket as a peace offering until the quiet you deserve is restored."

- "Pardon our appearance. Please take another look in two weeks. You'll like what you see!"

- "During our extensive renovations, Highway Diner will close one section at a time so our customers won't have to miss out on our great food and service. We look forward to continuing to serve you."

Perfect Announcement Mindsets

■ Closing a location is difficult for your employees, your customers, and your community.

■ When closing a location, don't just go quietly into the night. Thank your community and customers.

■ Thanking the town and the customers helps those who've worked with you feel that their business was appreciated and that you valued being a part of the community.

■ All change affects many people in a ripple that reaches beyond what most of us anticipate. Think of the relationships that you've built and that your staff has built on your behalf.

■ If you're closing your physical location and moving exclusively to an online storefront or presence, focus on the positive. Even if your reasons are financial, you and your customers will find numerous benefits from the change. Focus on those.

■ Sometimes the relocation is not too far for existing customers or clients to follow. If you're moving to a new physical location that still would be a potentially feasible distance for your existing customers, promote the new location. Give people a reason to go out of their way to visit.

■ When you know that your customer or client base can't physically follow to visit your new location, market via the Internet. Announce your Internet presence loudly and clearly.

- Adding a location is always cause for celebration and not only deserves a big announcement but also promotions that will help you spread the word.

- When relocating, announce not only the move and the new features your move will allow, but also think about draws of your new location such as a museum, a zoo, a concert hall, or complementary businesses.

- Stress the ease of travel to your new location.

Phrases

- "We're blowing the doors—and the walls, too—off your shopping experience! We're changing our location to an online-only storefront, so your shopping experience will be more convenient than ever! No more store hours, no more traffic, no more warehouse limitations. Visit us online today!"

- "Paper and Pen is closing its U.S. stores, but don't write us off! We've made a lot of friends here and appreciate your gracious hospitality during our 35 years in these outstanding communities. We hope to see you in our online store and in the Paper and Pen Pals forum. Sincerely, Morgan Terry, Paper and Pen President, and our entire Paper and Pen team."

- "Thank you, Westfield, for your years of patronage. We enjoyed meeting you, greeting you, and serving you. We will miss our friends and the warmth and charm of this colonial town, but hope that you will visit us at our new Manhattan location."

- "We regret any inconvenience the closing of our Springfield store will cause our loyal customers. We will still be available to serve you online and in our central Plainfield location."

- "You'll love our new location! Come see us in the beautiful heart of downtown Seattle."

- "A Parting Gift for Local Shoppers: Buy any item at our store closing sale and receive a discount card to use at our other five stores!"

- "Jeff Haimes, director of stores for the Gottit chain, announced that Gottit will close four of its fifteen outlets during the next six months. Visit our website at http://gottitstoresonline.com for store locations, closing dates, and sales."

- "Our new location sits just outside the downtown area, adjacent to a beautiful park with free Friday night concerts."

- "Our new office is just minutes from the Interstate."

- "If you cannot follow us to Atlanta, please visit our website, http://emoryproducts.com. All the products that you've come to love are just a click away."

- "It is with gratitude to our growing customer base that HH Porter announces a second location on Mill Road in Berry Township."

- "Our new spa is a little way out of town, but you'll find the spacious rooms and peaceful setting well worth the drive. After your massage, relax under a graceful canopy of trees, walk the path through the bamboo gardens, and enjoy stepping out of the daily grind and into absolute serenity!"

- "We're moving our wellness centers to serve you better. Visit us at our new location in beautiful Savannah,

Georgia. All the benefits you've loved—and now with some *new* old-fashioned Southern hospitality!"

- "Visit our new location, right by the beautiful San Antonio Botanical Garden!"

- "Rick Moll, president and chief operating officer of Diad Corporation, a landmark in New Jersey since the early 1980s, announces that the company is relocating to North Carolina. Diad's 300 employees have the option of remaining with the company and moving or taking one of several severance options offered."

- "Though our business will no longer be here, many of us will be to continue to patronize the fine restaurants and shops we've come to love."

- "We thank you for 35 years of business, friendships, and local hospitality. We wish you well and will miss you all, but retirement and the ocean call. Our best to you always, Judith and Jack Jones, Jones Travel."

Perfect Announcement Mindsets

- Changes in leadership affect company image, employee morale, stockholder confidence, and customer perception.

- New management may result from natural or positive events such as retirements, executives moving to different opportunities within or beyond the company, or a merger or acquisition.

- New management can result from internal or personal scandal or unethical behavior. In these cases, announcements of new management must be handled very delicately.

- Any change challenges the status quo and leads to some discomfort. Communicating the new management's qualifications and goals helps assuage concerns.

- Thanking the retiring or leaving management for a job well done and citing accomplishments shows a spirit of smooth transition.

- Visibility of and direct communication by new management not only can lead to comfortable acceptance of but even enthusiasm for the change.

Phrases

- "With this seamless change in leadership, LP Money Management Consulting continues providing advice that counts for countless clients."

- "We welcome Warren to this challenging role. Although he is new to YM, his experience and success in running complementary businesses is well known."

- "We are excited to face the future and a new direction under the leadership of Riz Rasheed."

- "Without Warren Berg's steady hand at the helm during the past half century, Arbis Corp. would not have become the industry leader it is today."

- "Maria Esteban has worked closely with Will Manning for more than a decade. We welcome her as Senior Vice President of Marketing."

- "Montoro Corporation is pleased to announce the promotion of Jose Romano to Senior Vice President of Research and Development. Jose replaces Elise Morgan, who was recently promoted to Executive Director."

- "Myles White, president and chief executive officer of Metro Bank, will take the helm of Metro/Wynan, the entity resulting from the merger between Metro and Wynan Banks."

- "Manny Alegro, store manager for Wyco Co. in Smithtown, has been promoted to regional manager for Wyco Co. Northeast, serving New Jersey, New York, Connecticut, Massachusetts, Maine, and Vermont."

- "InvestCo announces its new president, Roberta Fisk. Fisk says she is thankful for the continued confidence stockholders and clients have shown, even as InvestCo has weathered some difficult times. Investors welcome Fisk, who is well known for reenergizing companies and finding new directions for renewed image and income."

Perfect Announcement Mindsets

- When announcing a new partner, state the partner's background and qualifications.

- Consider who should know about new partners and how soon they should know.

- People are more comfortable with change that they can anticipate.

- Give people some way to find out about who this new person is, as he or she now has a significant voice in the company or firm. (The same is true for announcements of new management.)

Phrases

- "Stafford Corporation is pleased to announce that John Bingham has been promoted to partner. Many of you already know John from working with him in our Seattle office or through the 'Tech Notes' blog he's been writing for us. If you don't know John, visit his blog or the discussion boards and say hello."

- "Link and Thomas announces the promotion of Rod Harris to senior partner. Rod has been with the firm for 20 years, specializing in family law. To meet and learn about Rod, join us for a congratulatory dinner in his honor October 12 at 7:00 P.M. (Find event details and Rod's bio on the website.)"

- "We're proud to announce that Beth Cooperson, head of the litigation division for the past three years, is now a senior partner. Through her contacts, insights, and innovative ideas, she has been a leading force in our recent change of focus. We are excited to officially welcome her to the partners' table."

- "Bob Weller, managing partner of Weller, LLC, announced the promotion of Betsy Stanford to senior partner."

- "Merrill and Company announced that Laura Smith has joined the accounting firm as a junior partner. Congratulations, Laura!"

- "Reid Conway, president of GIVMI, announced that longtime competitor Harry Myles will join the firm as partner. Myles has specialized in product liability litigation for the past 10 years, earning the respect of both colleagues and adversaries."

- "Jake Somers joins Britton & Fineman as managing partner, a new position for this firm that has grown exponentially during the past year."

Mergers and Acquisitions

Perfect Announcement Mindsets

- Communicate anticipated problems and planned solutions.

- Sometimes combining forces helps your company grow—or stay afloat.

- Communication is your best weapon against unfounded rumors.

- Communicate why you are merging, acquiring, or being acquired.

- Communicate the benefits of the merger or acquisition to shareholders, employees, customers, and other stakeholders.

- When you partner with a complementary product or service provider, make sure that you're in agreement about when and how announcements will be made.

- Always be positive about your new partner!

Phrases

- "During these rapidly changing times, HLH has decided that we and our customers would be best served by combining our resources with NKH."

- "Through our seamless merger with MD, customers and shareholders will benefit."

- "Arrow Corporation announces its merger with Litro. Allan Young of Litro assumes the CEO position of Arrow Litro, and Margaret Daly of Arrow is the new entity's president."

- "In a bold restructuring move, the principals of Amro Consulting have dissolved that LLC and created a new entity, Viron."

- "In order to better meet market needs during a changing economic climate, two leading architectural firms, Vision Designs and Horizon Lines Architecture, have merged, creating New Horizons Architecture."

- "Alan Smith, president of Biltmore Investing, announced a strategic alliance with Holland Annuities. The two companies, working in concert to meet clients' needs, now offer a dramatically expanded array of products for existing and new customers."

- "Olson Furniture announced a joint venture with County/ City Decorating that brings a new level of service at a remarkably low price."

- "In order to enhance our customer offerings, Macro has joined with Micro to expand the availability to customers of help technicians and designers."

- "The merger of IH Consulting and WM Training offers clients of both realms a broader range of services, including integrated options. *Training/Consulting News* enthusiastically welcomed WHIM Training to the landscape."

Chapter 6

Internal Announcements to Inform and Inspire

"The problem is not that there are problems. The problem is expecting otherwise and thinking that having problems is a problem."

—Theodore Rubin

Place a high priority on getting your news out internally to keep employees inspired and informed. Internal announcements share news, clarify positions, and provide information about events and company issues. When announcing positive opportunities or events, you can generate or support excitement and a feeling of involvement and pride.

The more you involve your employees, the more they will feel respected and appreciated. Keeping them posted, giving them feedback—and eliciting ideas and feedback from them—creates a sense of ownership in, and a cohesive team that cares about, the company's success.

Message of the Day / Week / Month

Perfect Announcement Mindsets

- In addition to keeping employees posted on important company issues and events, consider sending out a message of the day, week, or month in an online or print newsletter.

- Your daily, weekly, or monthly message might focus on one area or be different every day.

- You might choose stock updates, reminders about the current customer service initiative, thoughts of the day, famous or inspirational quotes, positive global or local news that relates to the company, company news, or good news submitted by employees—or you can mix it up and have a message whose only consistency is a positive thought for the day, week, or month.

- Messages that reinforce your company's mission and culture keep people focused in the right direction. This kind of message is usually best when it encompasses the current company priority.

- Never underestimate the power of a light message. Most people are energized by starting the day with a laugh or a smile, and sharing a laugh with coworkers is a great way to begin the day in a positive way.

- When considering your message, think about what you want it to accomplish and how the message can best promote that goal. Great messages are motivational, insightful, upbeat and inspiring, or just plain fun.

- Relevant quotes from leaders in your field or beyond can be especially effective.

- Solicit and include messages from employees, and give them credit for their contributions. You can also select quotes from significant comments employees have made at strategic planning sessions or other company meetings.

- Whenever you read or hear a great quote, write it down so that when you need a message, you have a store of strong choices. Great quotes are easy to find and will inspire, motivate, or just make people smile. You can plan ahead and have quotes ready to go, and also use timely ones when they fit your current focus.

- Depending upon your goals and newsletter format, you might want to ask a different department to provide a message for each newsletter.

Phrases

- "Good morning! Let's make it another great day at XYZ Corp!"

- "Thought for the day / week / month: You are the face of XYZ Corp. Smile!"

- "Quote of the day / week / month: 'Dreams come true; without that possibility, nature would not incite us to have them.'—John Updike"

- "Quote of the day / week /month: 'What people really need is a good listening to.' —Mary Lou Casey."

- "Quote of the day / week / month: 'Listen. The simple, quiet act of listening will make you uniquely valued in the world.' —Linda Eve Diamond"

- "This week's message comes from Laura Oats, director of marketing: . . ."

- "Only one week until our companywide goal-setting event!"

- "In his groundbreaking 1973 book, *Management*, Peter Drucker said, 'Only a clear definition of the mission and purpose of the business makes possible clear and realistic business objectives.'"

- "This month's quote comes from comments made by John Ragle at our recent Good Works forum: . . ."

- ". . . —comment by an attendee at last month's Customer Focus Group."

- "Our new look reflects our new message."

- "Going green will keep our reputation in the pink."

- "We're making changes to take better care of you! Read about our healthcare initiatives."

- "When the customers weren't right, they left. If we want our customers to remain our customers, remember the adage, *The customer is always right*."

Internal Newsletters

Perfect Announcement Mindsets

- The company newsletter is a valuable communication tool that serves multiple purposes, which may include informing employees about new products, services, and initiatives; sharing good news about promotions; announcing new members to the team; reinforcing commitment to charitable initiatives; announcing or reinforcing a companywide direction change; and motivating employees.

- Your newsletter can not only announce but also provide strong, ongoing reinforcement of goals, companywide changes, or a commitment to a charitable initiative.

- Use your company newsletter to announce and reinforce a policy change, product shift, or process improvement.

- Announce training seminars and other personal improvement or skill enhancement opportunities.

- The newsletter provides a forum for key issues and a place for visible employee recognition. Newsletters may serve to elicit opinions and ideas for the improvement of processes, products, and services. They can also provide reinforcement for mission, vision, values, and goals.

- Newsletters are excellent vehicles to fuel community service initiatives such as blood drives, food and clothing collections, and fund-raising walks and runs. The more your employees are enthusiastic and involved, the greater your contribution will be. This translates into better results for your cause, more exposure for your company, and employees who feel proud of their personal contributions and proud to work for you.

- Include a "family" corner that highlights family events such as the birth of a child or a graduation or other achievement if your company size is conducive to that.

- Use creative graphics, pay attention to color and style, and include fun photos from events. A newsletter should be informative, but everything doesn't have to be news—a newsletter can be fun, too.

- Above all, a newsletter should keep employees informed and motivated. If they are amused or delighted along the way, even better!

Phrases

- "Got a Bright Idea? Every team member has creative, innovative, inspired ideas. Do you have thoughts about how to increase visibility or earnings? Save money? Increase customer or employee satisfaction? Post your ideas on the Bright Ideas Forum. We're listening!"

- "Thanks to John Burns for his idea in the Bright Ideas Forum! John gave us a great insight on how to gain free advertising on popular podcasts. Thanks for sharing your bright ideas, John! We are pursuing the leads and having success. We'll keep you posted when we seal a deal!"

- "Welcome to the team, Shira Patel! Shira is new to our management team. If you'd like to welcome Shira to our team, her e-mail is shira@ourgreatbiz.com."

- "Going Green Generates Green! Another customer survey shows that consumers understand that going green may cost slightly more at times, but they're ready to pay so the environment doesn't have to."

- "You made the difference! Thanks to your generosity, we reached our United Way goal."

- "Do good for humanity—and get free cookies and juice. Our Meta Blood Drive is scheduled for January."

- "Our We Care food drive brings out the best! Thank you for contributing to our largest food drive yet!"

- "Smoke Out Program a Huge Success! We thank everyone who participated and congratulate those who used the day as a good start to a lifelong commitment to a smoke-free life. The group that organized the event will continue to have regularly scheduled Smoke-Out events and meetings to provide ongoing support. Also, visit the 'Success for Quitters' Forum online."

- "Fan mail! We're positing our positive customer feedback under a new 'Fan Mail' tab on the website. You may work behind the scenes, but those fans are cheering for this whole team—they're cheering for *you*! Thank you for all that you do."

- "Congratulations to Mario Romero and his wife, Annette, on the birth of their second daughter, Julia Romero. Welcome to the world, little Julia!"

- "Safety Training begins March 15. Be there and be safe!"

- "Read our 'Family Corner' to learn about your colleagues' personal 'bragging' items."

- "Our January issue features new products poised for 2011 launch."

Encouraging Wellness

Perfect Announcement Mindsets

- Reduce stress and improve productivity by encouraging healthful habits.

- Offer healthful options beyond bagels and doughnuts to employees.

- Provide exercise opportunities when possible, and encourage movement during the day.

- Have walking or standing meetings that save time and burn calories. Small companies may not be able to provide showers, but they can provide an area where employees can freshen up, change clothes, and store towels, deodorant, and a change of clothes should they choose to exercise outdoors during lunch breaks.

- Suggest walking across the room or hallway rather than shouting, wheeling over on a desk chair, phoning, or sending an e-mail to a coworker.

- Offer wellness classes or seminars.

- Encourage healthful habits to protect all employees and to show that you care.

- A friendly, positive work environment promotes wellness, and open communication reduces stress at work.

Phrases

- "We're taking a break from the 'pastry break.' From now on, fruit will be served rather than pastries at our Monthly Report meetings."

- "New covered bicycle racks are adjacent to the parking lot!"

- "Optional tai chi classes will be on Wednesdays at 7:30 A.M. in the conference room."

- "Stretch your body, stretch your mind! Whether or not you join us for morning stretches, we encourage stretch breaks. Stand up for a refreshing stretch to the sky, back bend, or toe touch any time—maybe you'll even start a wave."

- "Don't type your way to carpal tunnel syndrome. Pause regularly to shake out your hands, stretch your fingers, and curl your wrists."

- "No internal e-mail Fridays have begun. Our one-floor, four-thousand-foot office is hardly too large to require everyone to walk across the floor to share a message."

- "On 'Bag-It' Fridays, everyone is invited to bring in lunch for random shifts in the conference room. Rather than hurrying back to work after wolfing down your sandwich, salad, or yogurt, take a full lunch hour to walk, practice tai chi or yoga, or meditate."

- "It's flu season. We care about your health. Please stay home if you have *any* flu symptoms."

- "The American Cancer Society's Stop Smoking Today campaign kicks off nationwide this week. Those interested in learning about this may attend an informative seminar on Wednesday at 3:00 P.M. in The Lounge."

- "Please use the Wellness Suggestion Box to share your ideas for ways we can help you improve your health while at work."

- "Attention Smokers: Please do not smoke by the front entrance. This is not only unwelcoming to clients, but presents a health hazard to anyone entering and exiting the building. It also allows smoke into the building. Please use the courtyard. Thank you."
- "My door and my mind are always open. Share your ideas and concerns."

Company Incentives

Perfect Announcement Mindsets

- Small incentives have a big impact. Consider what kinds of incentives you can offer.

- Incentive programs may be centered around one area of desired achievement, such as sales goals, or they may take into account a number of areas. Incentive programs can be based on sales, quality, safety, goal achievement, innovative ideas, recruiting, attendance, longevity, or more.

- Incentives can be material rewards such as bonuses, gift certificates, or small gifts, all of which may or may not be part of a formal incentive program.

- Incentives can be visible signs of appreciation such as a bulletin board and/or online posting of Employee of the Month.

- Many online incentive programs provide multiple levels of cash value rewards. Many are based on a points system, which allows you to track employee achievement and allows employees to see what rewards they can enjoy by earning additional points and to make the choice to save points for larger rewards or spend them sooner for immediate ones. Actions that earn points (and how many points each action earns) would be determined by you.

- Incentives may provide employee recognition awards for service, performance, or achievement. Incentives may also provide recognition rewards for milestones such as years with the company.

- Incentives may be rewards offered for top sales, highest customer rating, contest winners, service recognition, or any goals you want to encourage employees to achieve.

- Incentives help motivate employees by giving them something extra to work toward, and they will often help to develop team spirit along the way.

- Place a poster in a visible place in your office or store announcing and congratulating the Employee of the Month.

- Create an "Extra Mile" award for those who go significantly beyond expectations, and publicize employees who succeed in going the "Extra Mile."

Phrases

- "We're proud to announce our new incentive program. Now you can earn even greater rewards for the wonderful work that you do!"

- "To all employees: Starting in September, senior management will accept one nomination from each department for our Employee of the Month."

- "This year, at our Annual Awards Event, GreenCo will introduce the category of the "Extra Mile" award. If you are interested in being on a committee to establish parameters for this award, please e-mail margo@green co.org."

- "I know that these small pins are only tokens, but they embody my sincere appreciation of everyone in our office. I hope you wear them proudly."

- "Enclosed are tickets to the local theater production this weekend. Please accept them as a show of my gratitude for your behind-the-scenes help in that most difficult negotiation."

- "We're offering a new incentive program to reward not only the great work you do, but also the little things you do that are above and beyond expectations."

- "We know you all make a point of contributing great ideas and promoting our business. Now you can make a point of it! Our new incentive program lets you build points and use those points for special gifts from our catalogue. Every new idea you contribute that we implement earns you one point; every new customer referred by you earns you two points. Thanks for all you do!"

- "Go online today to see what your points can earn!"

Congratulations to the Team

Perfect Announcement Mindsets

- Praise is always welcome. Although you hired employees to do a good job, letting them know you are pleased with their work is always motivational.

- When you bring in a successful account, launch a new product, or have a great month, remember that you had "wind beneath your wings."

- Your most accomplished workers need praise as much as those who are struggling to do better.

- Congratulating a team, a department, or a division builds everyone's morale.

- Don't bend over too far in singling out one person's contribution or creating ongoing competition for your kudos. Rather, find a balance: Team efforts and successes deserve congratulations and praise as do individuals.

- Congratulations can take the form of a letter, an e-mail, a posted announcement (on a wall and/or on the company website), a Post-it on someone's computer, a handwritten note, or a scheduled luncheon or dinner, to name a few options.

- Depending on the accomplishment and your company's style, you can create a certificate or buy a plaque.

Phrases

- "Congratulations to our outstanding sales team for landing our largest account to date!"
- "Congratulations! What an incredible team effort!"

- "Jimmy, our top earner of the month, brought in a new client demographic."

- "Congratulations to Ila, whose marketing plan has won the support of management. Ila will share her newest strategy at our Monday Morning Meeting."

- "Congratulations on leading yet another successful marketing campaign."

- "We didn't win the state award for Best Restaurant simply because we have the best chefs, waitstaff, bus crew, bartenders, or hosts—we won because you're *all* the best at what you do, and you work as a team to give our customers an outstanding dining experience. Congratulations, everyone—and thank you!"

- "Congratulations on a great quarter! In honor of everyone's hard work to achieve our success this quarter, we will have a celebratory lunch at The Downtown Café."

- "Please join the management team at Rainbow's for dinner and a chance to acknowledge our semiannual top sales, service, and support team members."

- "I received a letter from Liza Dowling, one of our preferred clients, praising Elise and her team. Congratulations Elise, Damon, and Cheryl—and thank you for another job well done!"

- "Congratulations to all who contributed to our new look! Visit the website to see your ideas in action. We appreciate your extra efforts to enhance our image."

- "We're losing no time when it comes to safety! Congratulations to the team for another year without one day lost because of a safety issue. More important, we're glad you're safe!"

Training Opportunities

Perfect Announcement Mindsets

- Announcements of training opportunities for staff should sound supportive, not punitive. These announcements should have a positive, inspiring tone.

- A well-trained staff functions more effectively and efficiently than one that hasn't developed skills and tools.

- Employees should know that training opportunities are part of everyone's development plan.

- External training companies have staff with the necessary experience and knowledge to make the training valuable. Some people are resistant to outside trainers, so it may be helpful in your announcement to mention some of the positives, such as the background of the company used or the fact that outside resources often bring a fresh perspective.

- Companies with internal training teams have the advantage of providing training professionals who fully understand the company culture. If you're announcing internally conducted training to your team, it might be helpful to have a tone that reflects the familiarity of the players.

- The best training may be one-to-one mentoring or on-the-job training by a supervisor or colleague. These pairs may be formally assigned, or there may be a more informal call to less experienced employees to request guidance and to more experienced employees to reach out and lend insights, advice, and encouragement.

- An excellent training vehicle is recruiting employees with specialized knowledge to share that with their peers.

- Encourage teams to develop segments for a company-wide training initiative, drawing on each one's strengths.

- Online courses are not only popular, but also effective. They may serve as stand-alone courses or as a good supplement to any training curriculum.

Phrases

- "We are changing to a new accounting and billing program that will affect all departments. To make this transition easy on you, we're providing software training for all who are unfamiliar with the new system. Please see your department manager for the schedule and registration process."

- "Learn how work communication can be more effective when fewer texts, e-mails, and instant messages are sent. Please sign up for Communication: Less is More, a seminar to help us streamline and keep our communications on track."

- "Our customer service keeps our customers happy—let's see how we can make them even happier with us! Please sign up for Advanced Customer Service Techniques."

- "A number of key skill development courses are now available online. Please consider which options will be most valuable for you. What are your goals? What motivates and inspires you? Where do you hope to be in the company three years from now? Whether you're interested in moving up or broadening your knowledge and strengthening the skills you already have, speak with your supervisor about creating the best personalized education program for you."

■ "Attention Team Leaders: Team-Building Workshop Scheduled for February 1! Register today!"

■ "We take pride in promoting our supervisors from within, and we're proud of the on-the-job skills they develop. We proudly invite all supervisors to a new series of specialized supervisory skill seminars."

■ "We are interviewing for two summer intern positions next week. If you are interested in mentoring an intern, please e-mail your request to Human Resources by Wednesday."

■ "Please check the Training for You schedule online for off-site programs that interest you / that your department staff would benefit from / that match your Individual Development Plan."

■ "To all senior account representatives: July is our slowest month. This is the time to mentor and assist our junior reps to ready them for the fall takeoff."

■ "The newest *Perfect Phrases* book is now in our online training library."

■ "Please recommend that your staff members work through this valuable online training resource."

■ "Training is a valuable building block for our company. Please review the catalogue listings for our in-house, off-site, and online courses and encourage your staff to become engaged in this process."

■ "Our newest team member, Ricardo, spent a year working in Indonesia before joining our firm. Ricardo has some excellent insights into the business culture of Southeast Asia. Please join him for a lunchtime discussion on Thursday at noon in the cafeteria."

- "Alan's team in Purchasing has developed an excellent seminar that clarifies Purchasing's methods and requirements, simplifying the process for all departments."

- "Because we believe in you, all training is tuition reimbursed."

- "Our training programs are specially designed to inspire, to inform, and to bring us closer as a team."

Perfect Announcement Mindsets

- Encouraging employees to attend conferences is positive for both the company and the employee.

- Out-of-state conferences can be expensive; however, a carefully planned budget might include one or two beneficial opportunities.

- Encourage employees to belong to associations and organizations related to their work in general and their specific skills.

- Suggest that employees look for opportunities to conduct workshops or give keynote addresses at conferences. Those options increase exposure and limit costs.

- Attending conferences with colleagues in the same field offers employees the opportunity to learn what others are doing and to improve their own skills and processes.

- Send a representative to a conference and have that person later conduct an in-house seminar on the issues raised and methods introduced at the conference.

- Attending conferences provides an excellent networking opportunity that could increase business.

- Consider attending conferences aimed at client markets as a vendor. Have a booth to highlight your goods or services.

Phrases

- "The National Association of Certified Public Accountants is seeking speakers for its 2012 Conference. For those in

Accounting, please consider what you might offer to or gain from this conference. For those in other divisions, please consider what tangential skills you might offer this group."

- "Edu-Toys will be at the State Teacher's Conference again to show our newest educational products."

- "Please call Sharon in the PR department if you would like to join her in hosting our booth at the upcoming trade show on September 21. She will explain the responsibilities and benefits of this role, which include the opportunity to earn bonus commissions."

- "I am delighted to announce that Lou Scott has been selected to conduct a workshop at the National Association of Engineers conference in Phoenix next year."

- "Congratulations to Marc Geller on his selection as keynote speaker at the Annual State Transportation Conference. Mark will talk about his work in building strong teams during a slow economy."

- "Please consider applying to speak at the fall sales conference. Your expertise would lend an added dimension to our company's message."

- "Miguel and Richard returned from the conference with some excellent, innovative ideas that they will share with the entire staff at Wednesday's meeting."

Perfect Announcement Mindsets

- Company events provide a sense of team cohesion and offer an opportunity for employees to socialize and network without the pressure of workplace responsibilities. Often good work relationships develop and excellent ideas surface from discussions that take place in the relaxed environment of an event.

- Some events may be for local charities.

- Events may serve as a thank-you to employees.

- Some events are company traditions that employees come to anticipate.

- Some company events include families and others— often for cost containment—do not.

- Company events are often most appreciated when they are held on company time, though some events are best held on evenings or weekends.

- When announcing events that are geared toward motivating and inspiring, use motivating, inspiring language to entice people to sign up.

Phrases

- "A number of new people have joined our growing company during the past several months. To ensure that both current and new employees have an opportunity to meet each other, we'll have a Getting to Know You continental breakfast in the second floor conference room Tuesday at 8:30 A.M."

- "Join us for dinner! IronWorks has bought a table for the 10th Annual Chamber of Commerce dinner. Please sign up online if you're interested in attending. We hope to see you there!"

- "Fitorama's Lazy Day Luncheon is scheduled for October 20. Take a break and join us!"

- "Artistic Tile's Family Fun Day will be in Lenape Park on Saturday, June 16. Come and enjoy games for all ages! Prizes for all children who attend."

- "Who says accountants aren't fun? Our company Beer and Pizza Tax Relief get-together is April 20 at Sorino's."

- "Pharmcore invites all employees and their families to our Holiday Celebration in the cafeteria on November 10 from 4:00 to 7:00 P.M. Join us for fun, food, and gifts, but most of all, camaraderie."

- "Our team at Hair for You Salon works all year to help people relax and look their best. To show our appreciation to all of you, we will have our annual Spa Day this year at the Red Door on January 10."

- "Since our annual company golf tournament has been rained out for the past two years, we are having a bowling tournament this year. Use new muscles! Have great fun!"

- "Melbourne's First Friday Jam will be in the cafeteria on Friday, January 6. Bring your musical instruments, your poetry, your singing energy, or your appreciation."

- "Bring Your Children to Work Day is September 25. BW Inc. encourages all employees to participate. Nieces and nephews, godchildren and grandchildren are welcome. Join us in making this a special day to educate and inspire children! In addition to learning what you do at work, children can attend a number of work/play sessions."

- "This animated / one-of-a-kind / exhilarating speaker has captivated / inspired / motivated / delighted audiences worldwide / nationwide!"

Chapter 7

Other Important Internal Announcements

"Research indicates that workers have three prime needs: Interesting work, recognition for doing a good job, and being let in on things that are going on in the company."

—Zig Ziglar

The most challenging announcements to create and share center around difficult circumstances and negative transitions, but these announcements are critical to keeping things as calm and steady as possible. Your employees and stockholders both want and deserve to be aware of major changes before they become rumors. Hearing about change from the source is always more reassuring. When the news is unwelcome, your openness and tone will be the way to create receptivity and a positive response, from simple acceptance and understanding to inspiration.

Perfect Announcement Mindsets

- Sometimes what once worked no longer does. This might be a good thing or a bad thing—better yet, it needs no label at all. Things change. If at all possible, focus on the bright side in your announcements. If the transition simply doesn't have a bright side, be straightforward but also compassionate in how you present things. Remember that transitions can be unsettling, and put yourself in the shoes of someone who will be most affected. If you were that person, how would you want to hear the news?

- When announcing mergers and acquisitions, understand that any union with another company can potentially threaten your existing workforce. Employees need as much honest information as is practicable and appropriate to share.

- Restructuring may result from external forces, such as changes in market demand, the economy, or the available labor force, or from internal forces, such as retirements, vacancies caused by other factors, or a shift in company policy, mission, or direction.

- In most cases, whatever the cause or result, your announcements to employees will differ from your announcements to the public.

- Restructuring or reorganizing allows a company to bring a new perspective, and, often, new leadership to the fore.

- Restructuring or reorganization is often received with mixed internal reviews ranging from "It's about time!" to "Why fix what isn't broken?"

- The way you present a new plan often determines its reception.

- The more inclusive you are in seeking recommendations and/or keeping people posted, the greater the opportunity for their acceptance of the change.

Phrases

- "As we celebrate 20 years in business, let's focus on a dynamic new direction to carry us through the next two decades."

- "We realize our new product line reflects a shift in our company's overall philosophy. We appreciate your support over the years and hope you will continue to be as enthusiastic about our new direction as you have been along the way."

- "Our new services will require that all representatives attend additional training. We also need volunteers to mentor some additional team members we'll be bringing in to help as we expand. We appreciate your flexibility and realize this will be a strain for the first few months, but we believe this change is necessary for us to survive and thrive. Thank you for your help during this challenging time of new beginnings!"

- "More than a few clients have commented on our 'old-fashioned approach to problems.' This is a wake-up call we cannot ignore."

- "While top-down management has been our hallmark, we are eager to explore other models."

- "Our small team has functioned well during our early growth, but now we must add a new level of management."

- "In order to realize a robust bottom line, we must reinvent our image."

- "Our bank has informed us that maintaining our line of credit at its current ceiling requires us to cut expenses by 15 percent. We have two options: lower the ceiling or cut expenses. We are working to resolve this issue over the next few months and will keep you apprised."

- "Please look carefully at your department budget. First cuts must be non-personnel. Then we'll make a decision about our options."

- "With mixed emotions, I must announce that Diad Corporation is relocating in six months to North Carolina. The excitement of the move and the potential that it offers our growing customer base and our stockholders is tempered by the realization that this action will cause the members of our company family to face difficult decisions."

- "We encourage employees to join us as we relocate. Our Human Resources staff is available to explain both relocation packages and a variety of severance options for those who cannot join us."

Changes in Policy

Perfect Announcement Mindsets

- New policies should be announced, posted, and repeated. They should be added to the company network or intranet, sent in a formal letter, and/or e-mailed. Complex rules should be explained with a presentation, whether in person, video, or virtual.

- Post reminders. New habits take time.

- Any repercussions for not following the rules should be clearly stated in writing. No one should be penalized for not knowing a new rule yet. Consider offering a warning instead of a penalty as people become used to the new rule.

- Be fair and equitable with the warning system. If one person has been warned three times and another is written up for the first infringement, it will create unnecessary tension and bad feelings.

- If safety is an issue, penalties should be immediate and firmly enforced.

- Unless breaking the rule causes a serious problem, penalties aren't always necessary.

- New rules can be instituted gently, without threat of penalties, but penalties can be assigned, if necessary, if people aren't following the rule.

Phrases

- "New Cell Phone Policy: Cell phones may not be used on the sales floor. The focus on the floor is the customers!"

- "Please turn off your cell phone when you come into work. Notify anyone who might have an emergency and need to reach you during work hours to call the main number. Our operators / call center / floor supervisor / store manager will find you immediately."

- "Please restrict smoking to the designated smoking area in the courtyard. When smokers leave that area, they are too close to the building and smoke comes in through the windows and becomes an indoor health hazard. We want to continue to provide an outdoor smoking area, as requested, but we will not be able to allow smoking at all on the premises if anyone continues to smoke near the building."

- "Reminder: The parking area in front of the building is for clients only. Please park in the back lot. Thank you."

- "Warning: Cars without visible parking tags will be TOWED as of Monday, March 18. Please make sure your sticker is placed visibly in your windshield. If you need a replacement tag, please go to the main office this week before the new policy goes into effect. We're sorry for the inconvenience, but too many people use our lot for free parking while they go elsewhere, and they're taking spots meant for you and for our customers. Thank you for your cooperation."

- "Dress code: We love casual comfort, but some have gone beyond business casual. Let's put the 'business' back in 'business casual,' which doesn't include jeans, baseball caps, sweatpants, sweatshirts, or T-shirts."

- "Please read and sign your copy of our new Computer Use Policy. We need to know that everyone understands the new rules regarding downloading files, installation of software, confidentiality, prohibited use, and disciplinary action. Thank you for your cooperation."

■ "Business Expense Reminder: The company will continue to reimburse employees for business and travel expenses, but please remember that our accountants cannot allow estimates; you must submit receipts for all expenses."

■ "New Drug and Alcohol Policy: Due to recent events, we're strengthening our drug and alcohol policy for the benefit of our employees and customers. Any employee involved in the unlawful use, sale, manufacturing, dispensing, or possession of controlled substances, illicit drugs, or alcohol on LOV premises or worksites, or working under the influence of such substances, will be subject to disciplinary action up to and including dismissal and referral for prosecution."

■ "Telecommuting Reminder: Telecommuting requires being reachable! Working off-site is fine, but remember our telecommuting guidelines. If any employee does not follow these guidelines, we will no longer be able to afford the telecommuting option to that person. Our telecommuting program was developed at your request. Let's work together to make it a success!"

Perfect Announcement Mindsets

- Many companies hire people to represent them on social networking sites. Many CEOs and company representatives also blog, tweet, and link themselves.

- Unfortunately, some exuberant employees will write online about or represent your company in ways you wouldn't want them to.

- Without clearly announced guidelines, employees may defend the company in inappropriate ways, use foul language while representing your company, or use deceptive practices either for the perceived good of the company or for personal gain.

- Everyone needs to know that faked comments or reviews are not acceptable.

- Confidentiality agreements used to need less attention than they do now. People were less likely to break them over dinner with friends than they are now to pop company matters out online with hardly a second thought or, worse, to post under an assumed name. Anonymity online leads to surprising behaviors: *don't be surprised!*

- Clear guidelines for social media representation are essential. Employees should have these rules in writing and know how important they are, why they're in place, and what the consequences will be if they are broken.

- The big social networking sites may be great for big exposure, but some targeted sites might be as useful or more so for your purposes.

- You may or may not have policies that address employee conduct on social networking sites, and you may or may not (with legal counsel) address what employees post when not directly associating themselves with your name, but it's imperative to address how they conduct themselves when associated with your name or referring to you in any way—even under other names.

Phrases

- "If you write anything about the XY Company, you must fully disclose your identity and employment with us."

- "Please do not, under *any* name, insult our competition. Your credibility will be questioned, and so will ours."

- "If you state an opinion in regard to X Company or our industry, clarify that this is your personal opinion. We would never ask you not to express your personal opinion, but it must be absolutely clear that a personal statement does not speak for the company. Too often people take personal statements as company announcements."

- "Never, in any social media where you post anything about our company or your name is linked with us, use profanity, disrespectful language, or dishonest practices."

- "We have had a breach of confidentiality online. Remember that all rules of confidentiality still apply online, even though social networking seems so casual. No matter what you're communicating about, be vigilant not to refer to clients, and do not disclose sensitive information. Breaking these rules will result in immediate dismissal. We appreciate the excitement our employees have for the company. At the same time, we must all keep to the Code of Cyber Contact that is posted online. Thank you for your cooperation."

- "We appreciate that our employees are so proactive in spreading our good news! We ask that you please remember, at all times, our rules of full identity disclosure, cyber civility, and company confidentiality. Thank you for all that you do!"

- "We do not allow use of personal social networking sites during work time, but anyone is welcome to go to our business networking site and add comments, as long as it does not distract from other priorities. We all know how addictive those sites can be!"

- "Remember, whether you comment during or after work hours, you are still a representative of the company and required to follow all guidelines."

- "Please review and sign our social networking guidelines so that we know you've read them and agree to comply. If you have any questions, we'll be happy to answer them. Though we trust each of you, these guidelines are necessary for any company, even with the most trusted employees. Thank you for your cooperation."

- "We see worth in social media and appreciate the valuable team member contributions in our name; however, too much time is lost to online posting. We would like to maintain a loose policy, but we all need to do a good job of self-monitoring so we can have the advantages without a negative impact. Otherwise, we'll have to engage formal policies. Thanks for all you do to make this workplace both fun *and* productive."

Perfect Announcement Mindsets

- Specific company problems—financial issues, recalls, scandal, or the appearance of scandal—affect employees. During a crisis, assure employees that while you know that this will be a stressful time for everyone, you appreciate their calm, empathetic assistance to customers and their focus on customer care, even under the most trying circumstances.

- Employees should be coached in how to handle each complaint, no matter how rude or irate the caller, with sensitivity and understanding. Make it clear to all employees that if customers become abusive, they should be politely referred to a supervisor.

- Employees relate to the company; company problems— whether or not they directly impact employees—still affect them.

- Difficult economic times affect most businesses. Sometimes the negative is the most important news, and a positive spin would seem thoughtless. But put a positive light on announcements whenever possible and appropriate. There are, however, times when tough realities call for tough announcements. In a bad economy, it's easy to be open about your situation because so much of the country is in the same boat.

- Clients and customers will feel employee discomfort, even when employees try hard to put on a good face.

- Provide small incentives and rewards if you can to raise morale during tough times.

- Assure all employees that management shares their concerns and is there to help everyone through the difficult situation.

- Use humor—when appropriate, of course—to lighten the mood. Use it liberally and encourage it. Laughter isn't a sign of goofing off. It's a healthy sign that people are feeling lively. This is good for the personal wellness of your team and their effectiveness on the job, too.

- When employee morale is low, when hours are tough and money is tight, take the three most powerful no-cost actions for raising morale: (1) Listen. (2) Empathize. (3) Care.

Phrases

- "Customers who call will be angry and upset about the recall. Please stay calm, understanding, and polite. Explain the situation and necessary procedures. Should customers not be satisfied with your response, please refer them to your supervisor."

- "Our practice of annual salary increases beyond cost-of-living adjustments has always been the result of sharing the fruits of a good year. We appreciate your understanding that, as we get through this difficult year, we only can offer this base increase. Between our belt-tightening and your exemplary work, we expect to share in strong profits again in the coming year."

- "We know how disappointing it is not to get the bonus you deserve. We are doing our best to avoid layoffs, so we hope that you understand our position and that we sincerely wish we could give those bonuses to you."

- "Our goal is to keep our entire staff employed during these challenging times. We value each and every one of you and the talents you bring to the team."

- "Unfortunately, good years have been scarce recently, but we are pleased that we are able to maintain cost-of-living increases this year."

- "In keeping with the times of carefully watching costs while still enjoying time with workplace friends and colleagues, our annual company luncheon will be at Roma's Pizza this year."

- "As a small contribution to the economic stimulus, we include a gift certificate to Depp's Department Store with every paycheck. Happy shopping!"

- "Although we cannot increase paychecks right now, we can ease your stress by giving you a paid three-day weekend during July or August. Please schedule your chosen date with Personnel."

- "I'm sure everyone understands that overtime is not an option for the next several months. By eliminating this growing expense, we can maintain our current staff."

- "In order to minimize our employees' out-of-pocket costs this month, we are instituting Monday lunches in. We will provide food from Corner Feasts."

- "We realize these are difficult times for everyone. Our wellness partners are available to counsel anyone here at no cost to you. We care about your well-being and want to do what we can to help you and your families."

- "We realize that everyone has seen the news. Our outspoken CEO has ruffled some feathers. As we work on damage control, we ask everyone to stay focused on our customers and on doing the best job we can. When customers ask, please say that you're not able to comment on his statements and politely return to business. It may take a few tries. We appreciate your extra efforts during this time."

- "We're instituting 10:00 A.M. fun breaks. Anyone who wants to meet in the cafeteria for a 15-minute fun break, bring quotes, jokes, or poems. Everyone will have a chance to share at least one thing, and no one needs to share who does not wish to. You can come just to listen, laugh, and smile. There are only two rules: (1) nothing should be shared that could be offensive to anyone, and (2) items should be uplifting, funny, or inspiring."

Layoffs

Perfect Announcement Mindsets

- Sometimes the decision to lay off employees is necessary for a business to survive. Announcements of layoffs should be extremely sensitive in their tone and phrasing.

- Just as all change has a ripple effect, so do all layoffs. When layoffs are inevitable, recognize the impact on your entire staff.

- Those spared by what may be seen as "round one" will be nervously waiting for the next announcement.

- Even those who are not laid off are affected. A leaner workforce means a larger workload for those who remain.

- Anticipate and address frustration caused by all of these factors. Be honest; be fair.

- In hard times, it's natural to feel sadness and fear, and these feelings shouldn't be undermined. Don't announce the positive or express a positive, hopeful tone about the future without first genuinely empathizing and letting emotions, which are natural and necessary, settle down.

- Many companies have taken creative approaches to avoiding layoffs, such as requesting that workers accept unpaid furloughs. Some employees may be willing to make a sacrifice not only to save their jobs but also the team until the company is on more solid ground.

Phrases

- "We anticipate that within six months we will be able to carry our full workforce."

- "In order to keep everyone employed during this temporary, but serious, dip in income, we will hold a meeting at 8:30 A.M. to discuss options."

- "Even in light of recent changes in management and staff, I'm pleased to see that our company's sense of team is alive and well."

- "With sincere apologies, I must announce to our top management team that after 40 years in business, LMN must cut staff for the first time."

- "We are holding a management team meeting to determine how to recover from the impact of the economic downturn. We will look at all possible options. Our worst-case scenario, if we can solve the problem no other way, will be reducing staff by 5 percent. We value our entire team and hope that we will not have to lose any of you."

- "Before we approach the sensitive subject of layoffs, let's look at our current staff and projected retirement dates."

- "I want to extend my gratitude to each member of this team for agreeing to take one week of unpaid vacation time to avoid letting anyone go. Thank you. Although this is a difficult time, I know our team will come through stronger than ever."

- "As you all know, in recent weeks we've cut staff by 5 percent. This was a difficult decision for this company, and we wish we could have kept everyone on. Those who have left will be missed. I know that our remaining team is poised to carry us through these challenging times. Thank you."

Perfect Announcement Mindsets

- Safety is a broad umbrella that covers emergency procedures, protective gear, well-maintained equipment, clearly stated guidelines for acceptable behavior, clear consequences for not following these guidelines, and a reasonable process for both reporting and appeals.

- Encourage open communication about a safe work environment.

- Establish an open-door policy for questions, concerns, and complaints.

- Provide clear guidelines for a positive, respectful, and safe workplace, and announce a zero-tolerance policy for behavior counter to the guidelines.

- Be proactive. Address any behavior that does not support a safe work environment.

- Educate employees about the critical necessity of following safety procedures and of reporting safety concerns and violations.

- Provide a simple, easy-access policy for reporting incidents of harassment, intimidation, and other disruptive or threatening behavior.

- Workplace safety includes heath measures, personal hygiene standards, and a healthful environment.

- Safety protocols should be in place for natural disasters, and employees should be informed of them from the start. They should also be reminded of the protocols when a danger is in sight. Because those issues won't come up often, employees may not remember procedures. People can also easily forget things when under stress.

- In the wake of natural disasters, things may take a while to return to normal. People may have serious damage to their own or loved ones' homes, and utilities in some areas may not be back on as quickly as they are in your office. Employees are shaken and may also be dealing with injuries to themselves or family members.

- Urge extreme caution if your business is reopening while there are still reports of floods, downed wires, broken traffic lights, or trees and debris in the road.

- Set safety standards and announce, with thanks to all, when they have been met.

Phrases

- "Safety Check: Every employee must wear safety goggles when working in, stopping by, or walking through the manufacturing area. *No exceptions!*"

- "Everyone is required to read and follow our computer safety and ergonomic guidelines."

- "Cardo Company has a Zero-Tolerance Policy for abusive language or behavior. Should you have any doubt about whether a specific behavior or language use falls under Zero-Tolerance, assume that it does. This may result in discipline, suspension, or termination. Don't risk it!"

- "Our Safety Promise to You: At J&L Corp, all employees shall be safe from any language or behavior that threatens or demeans or causes anyone to feel unsafe here in any way. We will not allow threats, assault, bullying, intimidation, offensive humor, or harassment of any kind. Please report *anyone* in this company who violates this promise."

- "We do not allow jokes that could be insulting to anyone based on race, ethnicity, or gender. Ethnic jokes within ethnic groups are no more acceptable here than ethnic jokes about other groups. We need one clear standard. We all love a good laugh, but respect isn't a joke."

- "All employees are required to attend the following seminars: Preventing Sexual Harassment in the Workplace; Workplace Bullying: The Hazards and Solutions; and Cross-Cultural Awareness."

- "As winter approaches, we urge all employees to review the weather emergency protocols in your Information Packets and on our internal website."

- "In keeping with the local fire code, we will have a fire drill on Thursday at 2:00 P.M. Please treat this like an actual emergency."

- "The forecast for tomorrow is unquestionably severe. We will not be open for business tomorrow. Please call or e-mail any clients or vendors with whom you have on-site appointments scheduled and reschedule their visits."

- "Because our air-conditioning system cannot be repaired until tomorrow, we are closing at 1:00 P.M. today."

- "Hurricane reports are often exaggerated, but we cannot ignore them. Please listen to the early morning weather report and check our website before leaving for work. Our emergency phone will also be attended from closing today through closing tomorrow and beyond if necessary. As long as the phone lines are up, you can reach us."

- "Because of the threat of a serious storm, please bring your work home with you if you are scheduled to work on the Sensor presentation. We may have to work virtually, but we have to complete this project on time."

- "Following safety regulations is mandatory. We value your safety. Please do the same!"

- "Zero accidents is our goal. Submit your idea for safety improvement. The company president will host a luncheon for all who submit viable solutions."

- "NCK Industries is proud to announce another year of meeting our goal of zero safety incidents. We strive to meet this goal every day and thank our entire team for taking an active role in the ongoing creation and refinement of safety processes, their adherence to safety regulations, and their commitment to keeping NCK a safe, healthy work environment."

Perfect Announcement Mindsets

- We all want to know how we're doing. Sometimes we think we know—and we're incorrect.

- Putting feedback in a framework helps employees, management, and business owners.

- Your company is never too small for a feedback process.

- Ongoing feedback helps everyone avoid unpleasant surprises.

- A clearly articulated process helps prevent perceptions of persecution, protects fairness, and helps people know how to do their best.

- If your process is a traditional one of top-down, one-to-one feedback, these sessions will be scheduled individually, but you can still announce to everyone the time frame and put out a positive announcement to ease tensions and fears as the time approaches.

- If you implement a 360-degree feedback process, promoting input from multiple sources, regular announcements will help to keep everyone on track and remind people of the guidelines.

- If you have two-way feedback—manager to employee and employee to manager—the manager might consider announcing feedback that was given to him or her or to the company and be open about the process of making changes.

- Feedback forums are another useful form of feedback. Forums can be in person or online, but they shouldn't replace the more personal process that gives direct feedback to individuals.

- Any kind of feedback should be accompanied by follow-up.

Phrases

- "Performance reviews will be conducted during the first week of April. Performance reviews are a great way for us to give you the positive feedback you deserve, answer any questions you have, and offer assistance and advice in any area that may be difficult for you. We offer performance reviews to better support you as we all continue to work and grow together."

- "Performance reviews ensure that we are all staying on track. We encourage you to bring your feedback and concerns about the company. Constructive feedback can help us *all* do our best."

- "In keeping with our Employee Performance Review process, all managers are required to submit their appraisal conference schedules to HR."

- "Our annual Employee Evaluation process begins this month. Once again, I remind all staff that the purpose of these evaluations is support and performance improvement."

- "In order to ensure that our three-person office continues to function at peak performance, I am initiating a 360-degree performance review process. Let's meet to discuss what that means to each of us and to our company."

- "In keeping with our policy of continuous improvement, we will conduct feedback sessions next month."

- "Our goal of seamless delivery of services requires interdepartmental understanding of our processes and challenges. With this in mind, we will have a series of interdepartmental feedback sessions next week."

- "We are launching our annual, company-wide 360-degree feedback initiative. We ask all department managers to pick up or download packets for their staff by October 1."

- "Our formal performance improvement process is wrapping up. Thank you for your contributions to the process!"

- "We thank you for listening to our feedback and developing plans to follow through with positive actions. We also thank you for sharing your thoughts, and we listened, too. We heard a number of concerns about the equipment breakdowns and will be looking into resolving these issues."

- "Ongoing feedback and coaching is for the benefit and success of both employees and the company as a whole. Let's continue to learn and grow together!"

Customer Service Reminders

Perfect Announcement Mindsets

- Customer service initiatives should involve ongoing announcements and reminders. Even when outstanding customer service is taught, modeled, encouraged, and cheered, motivational announcements from time to time serve to reinforce their importance.

- Even with the most customer-friendly staff, anyone can have a bad day, and everyone can use a friendly reminder now and then.

- When a customer complains about an issue, an announcement restating policy should be made.

- When great customer feedback comes, announce your appreciation.

- Whether employees come in direct contact with clients and customers regularly or not, everyone should be conscious of always creating the best customer experience possible.

- Every employee should know how to deal with customers who are upset. They should also be empowered to deal with issues that arise on a regular basis and know when to forward customers to a manager or another department.

- Employees must be prepared to deal with angry customers, but they should know that they can draw the line at foul language.

- Employees who feel trusted, valued, and empowered are eager to do a great job and do their best to offer outstanding customer service. Make sure your employees have the training they need and open channels to ask questions.

Phrases

- "The customer is not always right, but the customer is still the customer—not only that, the customer is a human being who wants to feel that someone cares."

- "When customers are upset, do three things: (1) Listen. (2) Validate. (3) Empathize. You can only calm the situation, solve the problem, and even turn it into a positive outcome if you take these first three steps."

- "Announcing our Service Award Contest. At the end of each month, we will look at customer service ratings and write-in comments and reward our Top Service Star for the month. We will also take into account our interactions with customers and difficult issues. We know it isn't always easy, and we appreciate your patience and your spirit of service!"

- "Because our customers have been sharing so much positive feedback, we're going to make a customer feedback page on the website. Where your name is used with thanks and appreciation, it will be linked to your profile page so that others will see the great work that you do."

- "Do you know . . . ? None of us has all the answers, but if you feel unable to fulfill certain customer requests or if you wish you were better informed on some things customers ask about, bring your questions to Friday morning's meeting. Our focus will be customer care.

Bring your suggestions, too, for how to enhance our service for even better customer care."

- "We had a customer service incident over a $10 coupon recently, and the manager could not be reached to handle the situation. As a result, we are coming up with a new system to empower everyone to respond proactively to complaints and disputes within certain amounts. We welcome your input at a meeting to discuss and refine policies on April 11 at 10:00 A.M."

- "Customer care is our number one goal. Selling our products and services is number two. If we keep customer service in the forefront of our minds, we will naturally sell more."

- "Our customer surveys consistently show that our customer service initiatives are working. We thank you for taking our philosophy and putting it into actions that make all the difference for our customers and our company. Thank you!"

- "Our new system is difficult for clients to understand. Let's hold a meeting to share ideas, responses, and troubleshooting tricks."

- "Even the most difficult situations can be turned around. Go beyond resolving the issue to restoring customer satisfaction and confidence!"

- "NSA is committed to outstanding customer care, and we have just the team to meet that commitment!"

Chapter 8

Personnel Announcements

"The key for us, number one, has always been hiring
  very smart people."

—Bill Gates

Some personnel announcements target public audiences through media outlets such as newspapers, magazines, trade journals, websites, blogs, and tweets. These are designed to let clients, customers, shareholders, and other existing or potential stakeholders know of a positive change within your company. Others target the company's employees. These are internal marketing pieces designed to maintain a positive climate and create one of acceptance for those joining the company or being promoted within it.

Perfect Announcement Mindsets

- Changes in personnel within your company affect others within the department or division, those in departments or divisions who work with the one facing the change, and clients and customers.

- Bringing in new energy may be necessary, but the need is not always evident to those immersed in the day-to-day issues.

- Remember that any addition to a team or unit changes its dynamic. Any new person, in any role, affects all others in some way.

- Evaluate your need and plan your objectives carefully before seeking a new hire.

- Word your ad, whether online, in print, or through an agency, objectively and clearly.

- Consider an in-house posting before reaching beyond your company team.

- Be as clear and detailed as possible about responsibilities, expectations, requisite skills, education, hours, and any other detail that will define the position and streamline the process by inviting in only the most appropriate applicants.

Phrases

- "Are you an experienced human resources professional looking for a creative work environment? We're looking for you!"

- "Are you seeking a challenging but rewarding work environment? Working with disadvantaged families is challenging, but the rewards of giving are immeasurable."

- "We are fast paced, results oriented, and sometimes a bit frantic. We achieve results and compensate well, but we're a small company working in a competitive industry. If you're the kind of person who can stay calm in the eye of a storm, we need you!"

- "XYZ is looking for managers with strong leadership skills and a passion for inspiring others. We offer a competitive salary and benefits. If you have managerial experience and you're inspired to inspire, call today!"

- "AZ: A company you can grow with. Apply today!"

- "At Miracle Company, we're expanding our Human Resources Department. Following are requisite skills and experience: . . . ."

- "To all YK employees: We seek qualified applicants for our management training program. Do you know someone who's qualified? If we hire your referral, we will say *Thank You* with a $50 Universal Gift Certificate (good at hundreds of stores)!"

- "Please check our website for job qualifications and applications."

- "Our first priority is to promote from within."

- "Previous, related experience is essential."

- "Experience is not necessary; only an eagerness to learn and a friendly disposition are required."

- "The customer service representative will be responsible for taking phone calls and answering e-mails, maintaining records, resolving issues, and providing outstanding customer service. Each new representative is given a paid two-day orientation to learn our policies and procedures."

- ■ "If you're looking for a friendly work environment, strong earning potential, and a great benefits package, apply today!"

- ■ "Energetic, creative work environment."

- ■ "To join the BCA technical support team, you'll need experience, problem-solving abilities, people skills, and a lot of patience!"

- ■ "Be part of an imaginative, innovative team in an exciting growth industry! Sunshine, Inc. is a cutting-edge R & D company dedicated to developing sustainable energy technologies.

  "Requirements:

  - ◆ "Three-plus years of experience in the field.
  - ◆ "Bachelor's degree in mechanical engineering.

  "Responsibilities:

  - ◆ "Manage R & D projects from initial planning and negotiation to execution and final reports.
  - ◆ "Conduct lab experiments and report on them.
  - ◆ "Collaborate in the evaluation and selection of proposed projects.

  "Benefits:

  - ◆ "Competitive salary.
  - ◆ "Great compensation package, including bonus and 401(k) plan."

- "Servers Wanted! Winheart Hotels offers a generous compensation and benefits package. In addition to competitive wages, our benefits include:

  - "Medical, dental, vision, life, and disability insurance
  - "401(k) retirement savings plan; stock options
  - "Tuition reimbursement and ongoing training and development programs
  - "Hotel (room and food/beverage) discounts around the world
  - "Career advancement"

New Management

Perfect Announcement Mindsets

■ New management frequently leads to concerns among staff about job security, "the way we do things," priorities—how work will be different.

■ Promoting from within has its advantages and disadvantages. Stress the advantages.

■ Bringing in outside talent also has its advantages and disadvantages. Stress the advantages without belittling the current staff.

■ New management may mean that change is necessary.

■ Whether new management is the result of people moving up or moving on or a merger or acquisition, realize that your announcements are being made to people who are waiting to see how these changes will affect them.

■ If new management will continue to follow the company's former mission and goals, announcements should stress that. Announce what's changing, what's staying the same, and where there might be some flexibility. Communication is the key to employee comfort with and support of new management.

■ The company's mission and goals can only be achieved by strengthening trust, support, and teamwork.

■ Adding a partner to any organization affects the dynamic of the entire team.

- Stress the characteristics of the new partner that complement the strengths of those who are already in place.

- In announcing the new partner internally, state clearly the roles and responsibilities this partner will have. Everyone's watching his or her toes for scuff marks—make sure to assuage fears that the new partner will "step on current employees' toes."

- When you announce new management or staff, always thank the outgoing team members.

Phrases

- "John E., formerly manager of Sunshine Properties for South Jersey, has been promoted to director of Sunshine Properties Northeast. Congratulations, John! We know you'll be happy with the support you'll find here at Sunshine Properties!"

- "In line with Macro's new direction, we are pleased to announce that Marguerite Lennon will assume the role of vice president of Operations. Marguerite brings a decade of experience in helping growing companies grow stronger and adapt to changing times. Marguerite is known for taking an approach that's personalized to the company and team and for listening to the existing team before making any changes."

- "Our policy of internal promotions continues to produce strong company leaders."

- "Tsui Lin, formerly a team leader for the Client Services Division, is now vice president of Client Services."

- "Oval celebrates 20 years of successful design work for a growing client base by promoting three key employees to management positions."

- "Please join us in congratulating Deena Orson on attaining partnership status with B&L."

- "Nigel Bell, our new operations manager, has expressed a desire to bring this company back on track with its original vision."

Perfect Announcement Mindsets

- Recognize that any addition to the team changes the dynamic and may meet resistance.

- Don't "spring" additions on a working team if you can avoid it. Announce the addition(s) gently and with regard for the value of the team members who already are working hard together.

- If you need to bring in someone new, you'll find the best match for the team by soliciting input about the team's needs, strengths, and skill gaps. Whenever possible, include a group interview in your selection process.

- Solicit input from the team to find out where they sense gaps in the process and what strengths and qualifications they feel would make the best contribution to the team.

- Think about the "larger" team. Adding a member to a working team also affects others who interact with that team or support it.

- When adding to any team, consider the team culture and the best fit.

- Announce new team members in a way that will garner good feelings and support.

Phrases

- "In keeping with the team concept that has been working so well, we are adding one project manager to the department but are not filling the management position opened up by Pete's retirement."

- "As we've grown, our support staff has become overworked and overwhelmed. The best way for *us* to support *them* is to open two new support staff positions. We will post an ad and begin interviewing next week."

- "Although the Beta team has made great progress in compiling research, a thorough search and review of the published papers on this topic can be achieved on deadline only if we bring in an additional team member to help."

- "As general manager, I'll be interviewing new hires to round out our work teams. Please identify one member of each team to participate in these interviews."

- "Will Hecht will assume the leadership of the Capital Improvement Committee. The former committee chair, Lois Hanson, is transferring to our California location. We congratulate both."

- "Our newest department member, Jim Rollins, brings exceptional financial skills to the Human Resource Department. For this reason, Jim will be the department liaison with Accounting, effective immediately. I'm delighted to fill this vacancy with such a talented member of our team."

- "We've added two interns. They will rotate among departments for the first month. After that, we'll discuss the best permanent placement for each."

- "Welcome to our new team members! We're excited to have you working with us!"

Promotions

Perfect Announcement Mindsets

- Promoting from within creates a strong sense of teamwork and an incentive to succeed.

- Promote because of skill, knowledge, and accomplishments, not because someone "has been around for so long" or "really could use the money."

- When considering promoting someone from a line or staff position to a management or supervisory role, keep in mind not only the employee's knowledge of the job, product, or service, but his or her interpersonal and leadership skills as well.

- Promotions should be earned; they should not be "doled out."

- Promoting fairly promotes ready acceptance of your choice.

- Promotions should be announced widely and enthusiastically.

- The promotion itself may feel like a slight to someone else who felt he or she deserved it. Praise the person who earned the promotion, but be careful not to say anything that denigrates anyone else, such as expressing that no one else came close when making the decision.

Phrases

- "We are pleased to announce that RG, formerly assistant supervisor, will be promoted to the supervisory position created by LM's promotion to manager."

- "MB has been with the company for 20 years and brings not only invaluable experience and knowledge but also a clear understanding of our mission and values."

- "Jeffrey Jones, a pivotal member of the team that launched our successful online marketing campaign, now assumes leadership of the new Online Marketing Division."

- "You've all worked side by side with Mona Cooper for the past several years. I look forward to your supporting her in her new leadership role, replacing Tom Nelson, who was promoted last month."

- "I'm pleased to announce that two people from our department will be promoted to the newly created International Division. Congratulations, Max Fiske and Kisha McMoore!"

- "Donya has worked with KRZ for decades; she knows our culture, our goals, and those areas that need a boost."

- "Malik has led this team informally for years. His assuming the leadership role is natural and fitting."

Chapter 9

Reaching Out

"Almost overnight, the Internet's gone from a technical wonder to a business must."

—Bill Schrader

By reaching out beyond clients, customers, employees, and colleagues to your community and to other businesses, you enhance your company's visibility and image. Now you can reach out more than ever online through networking sites, links and affiliate programs, and ever-expanding interactive options, from discussion boards to opinion polls. Reach out to as many people as you can with your announcements, but also encourage people to visit you online or in person. As you consider your announcements, be aware of increasing your visibility in all of the places where you will post those announcements.

Opinion Polls

Perfect Announcement Mindsets

- Opinion polls show that people love to participate in opinion polls! Hosting opinion polls that are related to your business on your website is an enticement for people to bookmark to see the new poll and check out results of those in which they participated.

- You might choose to include commentary on the topic or poll outcome or simply to host the poll.

- You can use opinion polls to find out what your customers are thinking, what drives them, and what matters most to them.

- Some polls can be silly, fun, or marginally related just to keep your site interesting and motivate people to check back.

- When announcing or sending out customer service surveys, realize that few people take the time to complete them. However, the information you will receive from them is extremely valuable. Announcing an "opinion poll" may be more enticing.

- When results are important to you, entice people to participate and show your appreciation for those who do participate. Offer a small incentive if you can.

- Opinion polls can be formal or informal and can be via any medium: e-mail, U.S. Postal Service mail, telephone, face-to-face, or, most commonly, online. Opinion polls can contain yes/no or multiple-choice questions.

- Knowing what your existing and potential clients or customers think about your and your competitors' products and services helps you focus on your market's wants and needs.

- When conducting a survey or poll that is more than a quick single question, always say up front how many questions there are and/or how much time the survey or opinion poll is expected to take.

- Thank those who participate both before and after they complete your poll or survey.

- You don't have to know how to create an online poll or have a professional Web developer; you can find online sites to help you post and track Web polls.

- You can use opinion polls to encourage people to join your mailing list if they'd like to know about the results, future polls, and information related to the poll. This is a good way to increase your mailing list with people who are interested in your area of focus and might not have found you (or checked back) otherwise.

Phrases

- "Which of the following best describes your current lifestyle? _____ Very active _____ Somewhat active _____ I move when I absolutely have to!"

- "Cast your vote! We're creating a new look, and we want to look good to you. Please click on the two templates below to rate each option on look, functionality, and overall appeal."

- "How did you find us? _____ Referral _____ Online ad _____ Print ad _____ Other"

- "Please rate our service to help us better serve you!
  _____ Excellent _____ Good _____ Fair _____ Poor"

- "Please fill in the field below with any comments you'd like to share. We appreciate your business and your feedback. Thank you!"

- "How do you make most of your electronics purchases?
  _____ Online _____ Phone order _____ In a store"

- "As every member of this site knows, there are many good reasons to go vegan! Which is the primary reason that motivated *you* to make the choice? _____ Health issues _____ Animal welfare _____ Environmental concerns _____ I do it for my spouse/parents/another family member (or because they're doing it and vegan food is usually all that's in the kitchen)!"

- "This week's *This* or *That* poll: Chocolate or Vanilla?"

- "Where do you advertise most? _____ Online _____ Print media _____ About equally online and in print"

- "Where do you get your health information?
  _____ Popular magazines and televisions shows _____ News programs _____ My doctor _____ Family or friends _____ A certified nutritionist _____ Other"

- "Do you own your own home?"

- "Do you recycle?"

- "Do you have health insurance?"

- "Take our annual *Best of* poll! Click here to make your choice for the best businesses in town!"

- "What do you have to say about our service? We're listening!"

- "Please help us identify the services and products that best suit your needs. Completing this survey should take less than 10 minutes."

- "To show our appreciation, we will send a gift certificate / coupon for a 10% discount on your next product or service to all who respond."

- " Please rate our service using the following scale: 1 = poor, 2 = below average, 3 = OK, 4 = good, 5 = excellent. _____ Timely _____ Responsive _____ Pleasant _____ Friendly _____ Beneficial"

- "About you:
  - "How long have you been _____'s client / customer?
  - "How often do you shop / use our service?
  - "Do you use our facilities in other locations? Which?
  - "Do you recommend _____ to friends and relatives?"

- "Tell us about our products / services:
  - "What do you like most about working with / shopping at _____?
  - "What do you like least about working with / shopping at _____?
  - "What services or products would you like us to add?"

- "Thank you for participating!"

- "Interested in joining our list? If you'd like to know about the results of this poll and hear about future polls, results, and updates about insurance rates / real estate / travel deals / tech trends, click here to join our list!"

Links and Affiliate Programs

Perfect Announcement Mindsets

- Everyone seems to connect to everyone else's resources.

- Mutual arrangements to post complementary links on websites allow both parties to gain significantly greater exposure.

- Links through networking pages are more fun and friendly than ever.

- Networking site links can help you find resources with referrals by people you trust.

- Collaborative business efforts enhance all concerned. By developing alliances with like businesses, you can strengthen your delivery system, expand your customer base, and offer your customers more options.

- Developing alliances with complementary businesses attracts new markets.

- Alliances with like businesses may increase your product/service array and retain customers who may be ready to change to larger providers.

- One way to increase your visibility exponentially is to link to other appropriate websites. You may belong to a business or trade organization. Many offer to link member websites to the organization's site, helping you reach unexpected markets.

- If you decide to offer an online affiliate program, you'll want your announcements to entice as many people as they can. This automated referral system allows you to bring in new customers who might otherwise never have found you in exchange for a small percentage to the business or individual who hosted your logo on another site.

Phrases

- "Visit our Facebook page and link to us for fun daily updates and posts!"

- "Let's be friends! Link to us on any or all of the following sites where we regularly post updates and respond to customer comments."

- "Let us share our success with you! Join our affiliate program!"

- "Earn up to 15% for referrals!"

- "Becoming an affiliate is as easy as 1-2-3! (1) Sign up using our quick, easy form. (2) Place our logos or product photos on your website using the links provided to you as an affiliate. (3) Every time someone who clicks our link from your site buys from us, you earn 15% of the total purchase."

- "As a One-Stop-Web-Shop Affiliate, you can access our marketing materials to post on your website, e-mail, and online promotions. Link to our store and instantly increase the number of products you have to offer while earning 5%."

- "Click here to learn how you can earn passive income by promoting environmentally friendly products!"

- "Our affiliate program offers friendly, responsive service and top-rated tracking software. Click here to read more!"

Perfect Announcement Mindsets

- Customers appreciate the apparent bonus of a collaborative arrangement such as a restaurant discount accompanying the purchase of local theater tickets or a small vase of flowers provided by a local florist in a hotel room. Such collaboration gives the theater or hotel a unique touch and gives those local businesses exposure.

- For any alliance, no matter how short term, have a written agreement. Be clear about what you can and can't do and about your expectations.

Phrases

- "Biltmore and Holland clients will benefit from an expanded selection of investment options."

- "Dante Hall ticket holders receive a 20% discount at Angeloni's II on show nights."

- "The Downtown, Milford's boutique hotel, has partnered with the Milford Tennis Club and Shax Golf Course to offer discounted recreation to guests."

- "Spend $100 at our office supply / office furniture / printing company and get 15% off a one-hour consultation with The Ultimate Organizers consultants."

- "Buy a dress or suit at Mambo's and get a discount card for a pair of shoes or a handbag at Salsa's."

- "BeachFront Trust and the Foundation for a Cure have teamed up for the second annual Riverfront Musicfest, an outdoor festival featuring live bands along the riverfront. The event will raise funds for the two local charities."

- "As part of *Natural Planet Magazine*'s commitment to bring our e-newsletter subscribers useful information on new products, services, and educational programs, we want to share the following message from one of our partners, Beauty Cares Cosmetics."

Perfect Announcement Mindsets

- Initiatives in partnership with local schools, universities, and charities help your business and the community. Depending on the size of your staff, you may select any of a number of options.

- Company-wide initiatives such as blood drives, charitable collections, and participation in runs, walks, or telethons all strengthen internal bonds and external appreciation.

- Many companies encourage employees to donate time to local charities and to serve on community boards. Employees who do should receive recognition and thanks.

- Think of what products, services, or support your company can give, but ensure that the real and hidden costs are comfortably within your budget. No one wants to see your business suffer as a result of helping. It's as true for companies as it is for individuals that you can do more good if you take care of yourself.

- Schools and youth programs are always looking for people to share information about careers to show children and teens a broad scope of opportunities and possible directions they can consider for themselves.

- Contributing to the sponsorship of a local event might be a very small cost for the amount of good press exposure.

- You don't have to contribute to a local event to have a presence there. For a cleanup in the park, invite employees to participate and give them company shirts, hats, and/or water bottles.

Phrases

- "Metro Corporation is participating in the Fun Run for local charities on March 20. Run along and join the fun!"

- "Want to do more? When you sign up for the Fun Run online, you'll have an option to start your own page and invite people to sponsor you. Feel free to run away with this option. It's a great cause!"

- "So far we have 22 people signed up online for the charity run and private sponsorships are up to $725!"

- "Thanks to all who have signed up for the run!"

- "Levy's appreciates your business and is dedicated to supporting the community. Visit our website to see what we do to give back locally."

- "Building the Library—Book by Book! The library is seeking book donations. Bring your good-condition books to the conference room and we'll drop them off at the library on Friday, August 23."

- "Partners in Reading is a local group that recruits business employees to volunteer one hour each week to preschoolers enrolled in the Town Library program."

- "Take the afternoon off! Employees who would like to speak at the school career day or the youth center's What Can You Do? Career Day event, e-mail Beverly at beverly@commerceright.com."

- "Rock Solid Products is a proud sponsor of the local community service fundraising gala. The attached agreement outlines our donations of in-kind and monetary contributions, our understanding of our responsibilities, and our standard expectations of the charities whose events we sponsor."

- "Please call or e-mail with any questions regarding the attached sponsorship agreement."

- "We care!"

Seeking Testimonials

Perfect Announcement Mindsets

- Testimonials from clients and customers reinforce a company's positive image.

- Testimonials help potential clients or customers relate to existing ones and give credence to claims ranging from outstanding service to product benefits.

- Testimonials also offer clients and customers an opportunity for visibility in print or online. Because they give exposure that could act as a marketing vehicle for those quoted, you can encourage people to contribute by promoting that exposure.

- A client or customer can speak of your services in more glowing terms than you can—or at least sound more credible and unbiased doing so.

- Get permission to use client, customer, or company names. Some companies must run the requests through their legal departments; don't ask at the last minute when you're in a hurry to publish on a deadline.

- Many people will ask you to write the testimonial for them and show it to them for approval; do it.

- The most effective testimonials include concrete language that references benefits or service.

- Some options are more technologically complex than others. Do what is feasible for you. If you like an idea that might be costly, search for a simpler alternative.

Phrases

- "Please help us help others!"

- "Would you like to spread your good fortune?"

- "If you're happy and you know it, click your mouse! Click here to write a brief testimonial to let others know about your success."

- "For our 20th anniversary, we are compiling comments about our services, our products, and our employees for an online Anniversary Celebration Album. We welcome your comments and permission to acknowledge you."

- "Our new website will feature satisfied customers and clients in both print and audiovisual media. To be included, please complete the following form."

- "Adnil Company will be honored at the Chamber of Commerce Annual Meeting. We would welcome comments from our Advisory Board Members for the event program book.

- "We put our customers first! But don't take our word for it. Click here to see what people are saying!"

- "Are you happy? If you're a satisfied customer, send in your story for our testimonials page! With your permission, we'll name you and your company and even include a live link to your company website. If you're not happy, we want to know that, too! Feel free to call or e-mail or post your comment or concern in our public forum. We want *you* to be happy!"

- "*Can we quote you on that?* We've received so many positive comments on our forum, we'd like to create a Testimonials page. Please click new the new 'Quote me!' tab under the comments field if we can have your permission to use your statement on our site. (You will have the option to give a blanket release 'Always quote me' or a one-time release 'Applies to this comment only.')"

- "Nitch One's community outreach coordinator, Deena Horn, is a finalist for the State Chamber of Commerce's Big Heart Award. We know that she's worked extensively with you and would appreciate a letter that we can forward to the award committee, describing how she's helped you."

- "To those who offered to write testimonials on Mark's behalf, we appreciate your time constraints. If you wish, we would be happy to take your comments and draft a letter for your editing and approval."

- "How are we doing? Please click here to provide your feedback. Please check the box marked 'Quote me!' to fill out a brief form that will give us permission to post your comments. *Thank you!*"

Chapter 10

Purpose-Specific Nonprofit

"Never doubt that a small group of thoughtful,
committed citizens can change the world. Indeed, it is
the only thing that ever has."

—Margaret Mead

Many of the sections in this book can apply to nonprofits; in fact, some speak directly to fund-raisers and alliances with nonprofit agencies, but from the business's perspective. While those phrases and others throughout this book can easily be used or adapted for nonprofit announcements, nonprofits have additional announcements to make that are unique to their sector, such as seeking donations and asking for volunteers. These are the phrases that pay for a nonprofit's good work, so we offer them here to help the cause.

Additionally, businesses can gain from these mindsets and phrases for nonprofits. If you are in a for-profit business, you will find many of these phrases helpful for inspiration, motivation, charitable alliances, and more. Many businesses now reach out from the heart as eco-friendly solutions are becoming a strong part of our economy. Even if your business is for profit, you still will benefit from reading this chapter focusing on phrases oft-used by nonprofits.

Membership Drives

Perfect Announcement Mindsets

- If your organization has been around for a while, stress the longevity and successes achieved along the way.
- Always encourage members to spread the word.
- If you have a board that can help get the word out, ask for help. What can each person do? A small announcement from each person on the board on their websites or to their contacts beyond the organization can have a great impact.
- If you offer more now than you did before, reach out to those whose memberships have lapsed and tell them what's new in the way of membership benefits or the overall effectiveness of the organization.
- Announce the giveaway of a small item if someone joins during an event. It can be related to your cause, but it doesn't have to be.
- Use voices and images of current members telling their stories. You might even branch out your Web presence by allowing members to have special membership Web pages.

Phrases

- "Animals Now has been providing a voice for defenseless animals for over 20 years. Our campaigns have been responsible for legislative animal welfare reforms, and our efforts were behind the closing of the Big Cat Zoo, which was notorious for its animal abuses."

- "We love our members! If you're a member, spread the love! We need good people like you to help us spread our message of hope and continue to assist disadvantaged families."

- "We offer NEW membership benefits, NEW action invitations, NEW downloads, and all NEW forums! If you were a member before, come back and see the NEW www.HumanityGive.com. We're making a difference— come join us!"

- "Join Planet Earth Rocks at www.planetearthrocks.com for the most innovative ways to teach children about conservation."

- "Join us for our upcoming race for www.runfortheheart .com. You don't have to be a member to run, but anyone who joins that day will receive a special gift."

- "Join and let your voice be heard! Members can create their own membership pages to encourage contributions, show what they've done to meet the goals, and talk about their personal experiences with working for the cause."

- "Every voice, every ear, every helping hand makes a difference."

- "Global Links Human Rights is a new website that allows anyone to work from anywhere in the world to advocate for global human rights. Being a member, you have full access to letter templates, research, contact lists, forums, and videoconferencing with our directors. Members also receive discounts to special events, links on our website, and free downloads of our PDF information packs."

- "Our Members Only social networking site keeps you informed, involved, and in control. We offer a comprehensive list of "cause channels," discussion boards, petitions, personal fund-raising pages, and more! You can participate as little or as much as you want. Search information or become your own hub. We're changing every day so that together we can change the world. Join us in the evolution!"

Fund-Raising / Requests for Donations

Perfect Announcement Mindsets

- Show the need. Link to resources, provide pamphlets. Don't just offer generalities. Do the math. Make strong statements. Show the need for what you do, the need for assistance, and the difference donations can make.

- Make sure your website has full financial information about your organization, as well as lots of detail of what it is that you do and the impact you have had.

- Start with shocking statistics or current news stories that illustrate the problem, then invite people to be part of the solution.

- Tell what donations will buy.

Phrases

- "Animal rights advocates have won significant victories for Colorado's wildlife. Visit our website to see how much we've accomplished with our campaigns and see how your donation will be used in the year to come."

- "Voices Now is growing fast as we continue to provide free advice and affordable advocacy for low-income families. We are struggling with old computers and are unable to keep up with the high volume of traffic on our website. Please send your donation today so that we can continue to grow and provide these necessary services."

- "We are a community-based organization helping those with disabilities achieve their fullest potential. We inspire by providing special resources and job training and by inviting inspirational speakers who have overcome disabilities to be among the most able, productive people in our culture. Your donation can be the difference between despair and empowerment. Click here to empower!"

- "Love for Life is a charity organization that volunteers to bring pets, entertainment, and volunteers who care to hospitals and nursing homes. The changes we've seen as a result of our programs are dramatic. Visit our website to see stories and photos and consider making a donation. Even a small gift can help us help others restore their Love for Life!"

- "On February 12, 2011, the Global Peace Coalition will be hosting a silent auction fund-raiser in Berkeley Heights, New Jersey. We are currently seeking donations for the auction such as event tickets, gift certificates, artwork, antiques, electronics, jewelry, professional services, or other items of value."

- "Click here to make a difference today!"

- "Click here now to make a difference in a child's life!"

- "The Food and Drug Administration has announced that milk and meat from cloned animals is safe for sale to the public. In addition, the FDA requires no labeling indicating that these products are from cloned animals or their offspring. We need your help today to fight for our right to know! Join us and say NO to adding unlabeled, potentially dangerous foods to our food supply!"

- "Give today. Change tomorrow!"

Perfect Announcement Mindsets

- Say how many people you have volunteering and what others have done to help.

- State the responsibilities that would be expected of the volunteer.

- State the benefits to the cause, and also describe the personal benefits of volunteering.

- Offer as many ways as you can for prospective volunteers to reach out and sign up.

- Remember that invitations to volunteer must be motivating.

- Let people know how badly their help is needed, but don't make it sound hopeless or people will wonder why they should bother.

Phrases

- "Volunteering isn't easy, but heart work is its own reward."

- "Volunteers are the heart of our organization. Volunteers are the reason we've been able to help people worldwide and change lives for the past 20 years. Our volunteers are the heroes of this movement. As we all know, the world needs more heroes. We hope you'll join us!"

- "In 2009, volunteers donated over 8,500 hours of love to the children!"

- "We need volunteers with specialized skills, but also those who have the gifts of love and time to give. Please visit our website at www.cherishchildren.org or call 800-111-5555 to see how you can make a difference today."

- "Earth Movement is seeking volunteers to help with administrative duties, warehouse work, and event planning. To find out more about becoming a volunteer, please call our Volunteer Relations Coordinator, Bob Borley, at 888-112-1111, ext. 111, or e-mail bborley@earthmovement.org. We hope you'll become part of our dedicated family!"

- "Five-year-old international humanitarian NGO, based in Denver, CO, seeks an experienced volunteer grant writer to prepare and submit grants to private, corporate, and community foundations. For more information or to submit your résumé for consideration, please e-mail volunteers@ihngo.org."

- "Sisters Heritage Outreach Urban Trust is seeking donations to help young women through mentoring, empowerment, interview workshops, wardrobe donations, and child-care assistance programs. If you have a talent for inspiring, job or interview skills to teach, administrative skills, or business attire in good condition, call 888-123-4567 or visit www.shout successprograms.org to see how you can help. *SHOUT for a good cause!*"

- "We can't do it without you! Eco Lovers International events, activities, and efforts are all thanks to dedicated volunteers. We're seeking organized, enthusiastic, inspired individuals to serve on the board; assist with planning, events, and recruitment; assist with administrative tasks; represent ELI at fund-raising events; and more. Call 800-ECO-LOVE or write to us through www.ecolove.org."

- "Earthcor is offering great benefits to volunteers: connect with your community, make your voice count, use your talents for a good cause, learn new skills, meet others who are interested and interesting like you, strengthen your résumé, feel great about yourself! Call 1-800-EARTHCOR today!"

Engaging the "Next Generation"

Perfect Announcement Mindsets

- Encourage young people to participate. Let them know how they can make a difference.

- Don't talk down to children or teens.

- Provide resources for individuals, teachers, and schools. A young person might even find your resources online and ask a teacher to look into it.

- Young people are the future—and many are also active, eager, creative, and full of heart and hope—and will have more hope in the future if they start to join in good causes when they're young.

- Any organization doing good in the world can reach out to schools and young people. Vast numbers of youth networks and youth groups are also working with young people around the world.

- Take every opportunity to thank young people for their efforts and to spotlight those who have achieved goals or even set their own goals to help the cause.

- Announce your projects, links, and resources to teachers. Many will be eager to use your teaching materials and inspire children to learn and care through worthwhile projects—from letter writing or picture drawing to fund-raising to more complex individual or group projects.

- If you haven't seen projects, results, and even speeches by children who believe in a cause, you may be surprised by just how creative and moving they can be.

Phrases

- "The Global Net Human Rights Community announces a new resource wiki for college students to exchange ideas about how to use social media to spread the message, encourage student service and civic engagement, track campaigns, and have easy access to accurate information about worldwide human rights."

- "LIV is an international coalition-based student organization that works on social issues through partnerships and campaigns. We train students to understand the issues and reach out to other students. LIV—where the student becomes the teacher."

- "Kids Give is a community where young people learn, listen, speak, vote, volunteer, ask, and take action to make the world a better place."

- "Announcing our new High School Heroes Award!"

- "Teachers: Visit www.kidsecoweb.net to find great resources for environmental education categorized by grade from preschool through 12th grade. Kids will learn about biology, biodiversity, geography, oceanography, and more—and they'll have so much fun, they'll learn with eagerness and ease!"

- "If you think you're too young to make a difference, you don't know how powerful you are!"

Great Voices to Inspire

Perfect Announcement Mindsets

- Great quotes inspire.

- Be creative and use your own passion and your own great voice to inspire. In addition, call upon the greats who have spoken about your cause or about giving and community in general.

- In the nonprofit world more than anywhere, people need inspiration to give their hard-earned money or priceless time, to work against the odds, and to put the needs of others above their own.

- People want to align with great thinkers, and great thinkers add validity to a cause's ideals. After all, someone might have no respect for vegetarian diets, but may at least take pause at seeing that Einstein said, "Nothing will benefit human health and increase the chances for survival of life on earth as much as the evolution to a vegetarian diet."

- Look to organizers, motivators, writers, philosophers, and poets. These are people who know how to hone phrases, evoke emotion, and inspire.

Phrases

- "'Real generosity toward the future lies in giving all to the present.' —Albert Camus"

- "'The time is always right to do what is right.' —Martin Luther King Jr."

- "'We must become the change we want to see in the world.' —Mohandas Gandhi"

- "'The difference between what we do and what we are capable of doing would suffice to solve most of the world's problems.' —Mohandas Gandhi"

- "'You are not here merely to make a living. You are here in order to enable the world to live more amply, with greater vision, with a finer spirit of hope and achievement. You are here to enrich the world, and you impoverish yourself if you forget the errand.' —Woodrow Wilson"

- "'Every action of our lives touches on some chord that will vibrate in eternity.' —Edwin Hubbel Chapin, American Universalist Society preacher"

- "'What we think or what we believe is, in the end, of little consequence. The only thing of consequence is what we do.' —John Ruskin, English poet and philosopher"

- "'Start by doing what is necessary, then what is possible, and suddenly you are doing the impossible.' —St. Francis of Assisi"

- "'Regret for the things we did can be tempered by time; it is regret for the things we did not do that is inconsolable.' —Sydney J. Harris, American journalist"

- "'The greatest of all mistakes is to do nothing because you can only do a little. Do what you can.' —Sydney Smith, English writer and Anglican clergyman"

- "'Most of the important things in the world have been accomplished by people who have kept on trying when there seemed to be no hope at all.' —Dale Carnegie"

- "'If it's un-environmental, it is uneconomical. That is the rule of nature.' —Mollie Beattie, Director, U.S. Fish and Wildlife Service"

- "'What is the good of having a nice house without a decent planet to put it on?' —Henry David Thoreau"

- "'The love for all living creatures is the most notable attribute of man.' —Charles Darwin"

- "'When I hear of the destruction of a species, I feel just as if all the works of some great writer have perished.' —Theodore Roosevelt"

- "'An animal's eyes have the power to speak a great language.' —Martin Buber, Austrian Jewish philosopher"

- "'The animals of the planet are in desperate peril. Without free animal life I believe we will lose the spiritual equivalent of oxygen.' —Alice Walker, American writer"

- "'Each species is a masterpiece, a creation assembled with extreme care and genius.' —Edward O. Wilson"

Chapter 11

Thank You!

"The deepest craving of human nature is the need
to be appreciated."

—William James

"Thank you" is one of the most uplifting concepts and phrases. So many customers—and employees—believe that "the company" takes them for granted. Showing appreciation builds goodwill, motivates, inspires, and lets people know that you know your business couldn't have gotten where it has without the input, support, and dedication of a few or many people. Nothing beats a personalized thank-you; thankfully, though, a public, broad-based announcement of thanks, a bulk-rate announcement by mail, and a more personalized thank-you card all have their place as well and will be welcomed. Do what you can, but never be too busy to think of stopping to say thank you any and every way you can. These messages of thanks may be coupled with special offers or many of the other announcements in this book, or they may stand alone as simple statements of gratitude. Never undervalue the impact of an expression of appreciation.

Thank You for Your Business

Perfect Announcement Mindsets

- You can say thank you in many ways: letters, e-mails, newspaper ads, postcards, personal notes, gifts, and more.

- Many small business owners say thank you annually by sending a thoughtful birthday gift to loyal clients or customers.

- Some business owners will send or personally deliver treats at a holiday time.

- Offer thank-you discounts or a small free product or service as a thank-you.

- A handwritten thank-you card is worth a great deal these days. A printed, signed card is also worth a great deal. Just putting something personalized in the mail tells customers that they're worth the extra effort. If you send a preprinted card, add a personalized P.S.

- A thank-you card acts as an advertisement by putting your name in front of the customer as a reminder.

- Your style may be simple or elegant—what matters is that you took the time to say thanks.

- Your note can include a coupon. You can also streamline to make the note itself the coupon: "Bring this note for a special discount."

- Announcing your thanks online to all who have been your customers, all who have referred customers, or all who have given is also useful. A broad-based announcement still shows your gratitude.

- A thank-you can be expressed online after a purchase is made and included with a product when it's sent out.
- A thank-you can come with a request to fill out a customer service survey or a product or service rating.

Phrases

- "Thank you for your business! We're delighted that you've chosen our business / services. We look forward to working with you to make your project / event / venture a success."
- "Thank you for voting on the Customer Choice website to make us the number-one-rated spa in New Mexico!"
- "Thank you for continuing to be part of the XYZ family. Happy Holidays!"
- "Serving you is our treat. Please stop by during Halloween week for a sweet treat from us."
- "Happy Birthday! Another birthday means another year that we've enjoyed serving you. Please accept this coupon as a show of our appreciation. We hope that you enjoy your special day!"
- "Your order is en route, and I want to thank you for your business. Jim Watson, Customer Service Director."
- "Thank you for your recent purchase from Homestead Businesses. We appreciate your business and look forward to continuing to serve you. Tanya Smith, President, BU Products, Inc."

Perfect Announcement Mindsets

- Employee respect and appreciation are paramount to retention, motivation, and generating good feelings that will ultimately benefit the company.

- Employee thank-yous should be given not only to the team as a whole but also to individuals and departments.

- Nothing is more effective than an individual thank-you, but public appreciation for the entire team goes a long way in showing gratitude for everyone and fostering a sense of team.

- Announcements of gratitude for the team can also be online in employee posts, messages, and newsletters.

- Announcements can be hung in the office as reminders so people can see, in the midst of a long day, that their hard work is appreciated.

Phrases

- "Thank you for your dedication to our business / cause. We are lucky to have such talented, dedicated people on our team!"

- *"You* are the reason for our success. We thank you for your hard work and dedication."

- "Your job may be tireless, but we promise that it isn't thankless. We appreciate each one of you each and every day."

- "Our support staff has been outstanding during this sales campaign. Thank you all!"

- "We're rated number one in customer satisfaction. Why are our customers so happy? We know why—because of your hard work. Thank you!"

- "We are one of the top-rated companies in our field because we have the top professionals in the field working for us. We thank you for being part of our team!"

- "Thank you for another great year! Profits are steady, which says a lot in this tough economy. We appreciate your hard work and dedication to getting us through these tough times. Great work!"

- "Profits are up, *thanks to you!*"

- "Thank you for being the team that consistently stays on track, goes the extra mile, and brings home the gold!"

- "We've reached our goals! Great work, everyone—thank you!"

Thank You for Your Donation

Perfect Announcement Mindsets

- Announcements of appreciation for donations may be used by nonprofits, but they also should be used by businesses that align with or become involved with charity initiatives.

- Donations to a charity that you run are critical to its success, and donations to charities that your company supports are a way for you to help and to expand your reach into the community.

- Be sure to acknowledge all who participate either financially or in kind.

- Never ask for another donation in the same announcement or note of thanks. It undermines the gratitude for what was given. It says thanks, but couldn't you do more? You're more likely to have a follow-up donation by not asking before the person donating feels the gift was appreciated.

- The world is filled with takers. Always be thankful to givers, especially those who are helping your cause, and announce your thanks in as many places as you can. You can have a thank-you banner at an event, a special thank-you on your website, a thank-you gift with a thank-you message, and still follow up with a thank-you card. No one ever tires of being appreciated.

Phrases

- "Thank you for donating school supplies for disadvantaged children in our community. Your donation is helping to give children the tools to learn. With those tools come confidence and a world of possibilities. On behalf of the children and their families, we thank you for your support."

- "Thank you to all AXO employees who donated funds for the relief effort. We have ensured that every dollar you gave will have double the benefit by matching your contributions dollar for dollar. The final tally of donations by AXO employees and our dollar-for-dollar match was $_____."

- "Thanks to all who kindly donated raffle prizes for the Arts for Children fund-raiser. The event was a great success and raised over $_____ for community center art supplies. The raffle was one of the highlights of the afternoon and was responsible for a significant percentage of money raised."

- "We thank those who generously donated their time to make our Children's Health event a success. Time is the most valuable commodity we have, and we thank those who gave theirs so freely for the sake of Children's Health."

- "We thank those who donated funds and those who donated their time. Because of you, we held a successful event and reached our goal. We deeply appreciate your kindness, generosity, and caring."

- "So many people have good intentions to help and good reasons why there's never time. Those who find the time in spite of those good reasons are extraordinarily special, and we thank each one who has reached out to help our cause."

- "'The smallest act of kindness is worth more than the greatest intention.' —Oscar Wilde. We thank those who acted in kindness for our cause. Each person who donated money or time—in any amount—gave a gift that was priceless. Thank you!"

- "Grains For Life Food Bank has a new truck on the road to reach more children and families thanks to a generous donation by We Care Industries. We thank We Care for caring and taking action to help the hunger cause."

- "'Be the change you want to see in the world.' —Mohandas Gandhi. Thank you for being the change!"

Thank You for Referrals

Perfect Announcement Mindsets

- Post an announcement of appreciation in a public space to thank customers for referring other customers. It shows your appreciation to those clients and tells prospective clients that others have been so pleased with your company that they referred you to friends, family, and colleagues.

- Announce your appreciation of referrals in your newsletter or e-mail blasts.

- An announcement of appreciation for referrals might spark someone else to refer you who might not have thought about it.

- Offer a discount or free gift for referrals as a thank-you and to entice more clients and customers to recommend you.

Phrases

- "Thank you for your kind referrals! New customers often tell us they were sent by friends or family. The greatest compliment anyone can give to a business is to recommend it to others, and we're happy to know that you enjoy your experience here enough to recommend it. We appreciate your enthusiasm about our business and your faith that your friends and family will feel at home here. We look forward to seeing you soon!"

- "We're growing, *thanks to you*! Referrals have increased our business, and we're running a customer appreciation sale this weekend! Bring this announcement for an extra 10% off!"

- "Thank you for participating in our friends and family event."

- "Thank you for having the confidence to refer your friends, family, and colleagues to us! We appreciate your enthusiasm and trust."

- "Our business is growing, thanks to you! Our clients consistently recommend ABC Cleaning Services to friends and family. We appreciate your kindness and your confidence."

- "We appreciate your referral. As a small token of thanks, we will send a check for $50 to anyone whose referral becomes a client."

Part Three

Writing *Your* Perfect Phrases

We hope you're using and enjoying the phrases in this book. If you are, you've probably noticed that there's no magic to the "perfect phrase," only some perfect announcement mindsets and a few basic elements. These include a focus on your intent and audience, a positive tone, powerful language, clarity, and a little creativity. In Chapter 12, we offer a look at these elements and some inspiration and advice to encourage you to try writing your own *perfect phrases*. If you don't have a writing background, you may not be aware of some of the most common errors and how to avoid them. Chapter 13 gives you a simple "crash course" on avoiding these errors as well as a few proofreading suggestions. Whether or not you write or refine a phrase, you'll want to make sure that your final announcement is correct. We know you'll want to look *perfect* when you announce yourself!

Chapter 12

Your Perfect Phrases

"Creativity is allowing yourself to make mistakes. Art is knowing which ones to keep."

—Scott Adams, *Dilbert* cartoonist

I n this chapter, you'll see some of the elements that make a phrase perfect, then some simple suggestions for generating your own phrases. While putting out effective announcements is serious business, having some fun with phrases will often produce powerful results. If you're feeling creative, inspired, or just focused on generating the best, most targeted messages for your announcements, it may be time for you to play with phrases. In fact, some of your most productive ideas may come when you make it fun and relaxed with a friend.

Have You Made Some *Perfect* Notes?

We hope you will continue to use the *perfect phrases* from this book that apply to your announcements, to modify others, and to use these phrases as foundations for creating your own *perfect phrases*. While reading, you've probably already come up with a few of your own. You may have highlighted, tabbed, and jotted down phrases of particular interest to you to ingrain them in your memory and have them handy as you create announcements. Following the guidelines in this chapter, you will add to that storehouse of phrases the words of a great thinker in your industry—someone who knows your business better than anyone else—*you*!

What Makes a Phrase *Perfect*?

What makes a phrase *perfect*? What makes it meaningful or effective? What makes it inspire, motivate, or entice? There is no magic recipe to creating the *perfect phrase*, but the best ingredients for any announcement are words that speak to the intended audience and are appropriate for the occasion. Words that sell are strong, positive, inspiring, confident; words that brand your image in peoples' minds are creatively phrased in unique ways; phrases that deliver bad news should be sensitive and deliberate.

If you question the language or tone of a phrase, slow down and think it over carefully. If you fear it will be confusing or sound insensitive or convey a slightly different message than intended, then it probably will be interpreted (or misinterpreted) in just that way by at least some, if not a majority, of your audience. If you're questioning a phrase, you're doing so for a reason, so whatever it is that makes you question a phrase should be the basis for revising it. If in doubt, get opinions—ideally from a few people who are likely to have different perspectives.

A Perfect Brainstorm

Now let's take another step and brainstorm some new *perfect phrases*. The best way to keep track of your *perfect phrases* is to keep them in a notebook or computer document. Brainstorm your own *perfect phrases* for each of the following, making each bullet the heading of a page and adding as many phrases for each one as you can.

- The best first line of a press release announcing your next big news
- The perfect headline for announcing your new product or service
- The perfect way to announce your big sale
- The best first line for a motivational statement to employees
- The most descriptive, enticing way to announce your next event
- A great quotation about customer service and your perfect phrase to highlight how your company exemplifies the statement
- Great metaphors relating to your product, service, or cause
- The perfect motivational announcement to your team
- The best phrase to show gratitude to your team
- A great quote about gratitude and your perfect phrase to support it
- The perfect phrase for announcing an upcoming change to employees
- The perfect phrase for announcing the same change to the public

When you feel that you've run out of phrases, push yourself to come up with three more. You may be surprised by the creativity that surfaces just when you think the well is dry. This might take a few concentrated sessions. We also recommend carrying your phrases with you to jot down more as they come to you, whether later in the day or over time. Jot new ideas down, and add them to your lists. Keep these lists alive and active, referring to and adding to this book and your lists over time. You'll find that your new phrases will become ingrained, and your announcements will continually be refined.

A Perfect Buddy

Do you know someone else who might have ideas to contribute? Take your brainstorming to a new level by going through the process with a coworker or someone else in your field. Share your lists and see how many more entries you can come up with together. Write them all down—even the silly ones. The more fun you have, the more great, usable ideas you'll generate. Then you can practice your phrases, share them with your phrase-generating buddy, and see what works well and what you might refine. You don't have to make a job out of it or take it too seriously, but if you allow yourself to have a perfectly good time playing with phrases, you might just find an announcement that inspires employees, brings new customers through your doors, or becomes a great tagline or the heart of a new mission statement.

Six More *Perfect Phrase* Tips

1. Be Perfectly Positive

Most *perfect phrases* have a positive tone. As you develop and refine your phrases, use positive words and positive messages. Go through your phrases and flag negative words such as *no, not, aren't, can't, may not,* and *won't.* Can you rephrase with a positive tone? Think in positive words and positive terms. Is your success *not uncommon,* or is it *common*? The two expressions may mean the same thing, but cutting the negative words gives the phrase a more positive sound. Is your glass *half empty,* or is it *half full*? Is the buyer *half disinterested* or *half interested*? Are your words *not uninspiring,* or are they *inspiring*? Be *perfectly* positive for a positively *perfect* outcome.

Here are a few more perfectly positive examples:

- Rather than saying, "Our widgets aren't flimsy," say, "Our widgets are strong," or "The durability of our widgets is the backbone of our success."
- Instead of "It's not uncommon for our consulting clients to cut employee turnover by as much as 50 percent," say, "Our clients cut employee turnover by as much as 50 percent" or "Our clients retain as many as 50 percent more of their valued employees."

While it's easy to use positive language for good news, some news is harder to hear and accept. Still, you can put the picture in a positive frame. Here are a few perfectly negative, positive examples:

- You don't have to say, "Because of the tough economy, we're closing our stores and will now be exclusively online." You can say, "In keeping with the times, we're now exclusively online!"
- Don't announce, "We don't take returns after 30 days"; announce, "We take returns for up to 30 days."

Focus more on positive, intriguing words and a positive *yes* attitude. Reduce the nays, increase the yeas!

2. Be Perfectly Clear

Language is the stuff of which your phrases are made—use it wisely. Language involves a number of choices. The language you choose to communicate announcements should be clear and concise.

Make sure your wording cannot be read in more than one way. Following are some examples of announcements that lack clarity. They may get a laugh, but they won't meet the mark:

- "Help Wanted: Man to Wash Dishes and Two Waitresses" (What exactly is this man hired to wash?)
- "Don't Let Stress Wear You Down—Let Us Help!" (Are we helping the stress?)
- "Great Deals for Men with 16 and 17 Necks" (Those men have how many necks? Hopefully, there's a big sale on hats, too! A little word like "size" makes a big difference.)
- "Half off on consulting services today!" (Is that if I use the service today, or if I sign up for the service today?)
- "Milk Drinkers Are Turning to Soy" (Again, we can see what the writer is trying to say, but it just sounds messy!)

■ "Only one minor accident this year. Let's resolve to do better!" (Are we aiming for more accidents?)

Problems also arise when we use words unfamiliar to the listener, whether there is a language barrier or we are simply enjoying our new-word-a-day calendar at the expense of anyone who chose a *Dilbert* calendar instead. We also lose each other with technical jargon and Internet shorthand. Announcements can only entice, wow, be appreciated, or yield results when they're understood—and few people will take the time to figure out what is not clear at first glance.

3. Pack the Perfect Punch

More words often mean less punch. Be succinct and use strong verbs to state your message. Rather than saying, "Due to the fact that we're expanding, we're hiring new employees." Say, "We're expanding! Come grow with us. *Apply today!*" Avoid excess words of any kind; that will make the words you do use more powerful. Redundancy, unless it is used for a very specific reason, also weakens your punch. Rather than saying, "short in length," keep it "short."

Following are a few examples of using fewer words for greater impact:

Rather than	*Say*
Make a decision	Decide
Gave a speech	Spoke
Conservation of energy	Energy conservation
Blue in color	Blue
Assistant to the manager of operations	Assistant operations manager

More words don't necessarily say more; in fact, they can water down your message and say less. Per an old Polish proverb, "Words must be weighed, not counted."

4. Create Eye-Catching Headings

Your heading makes the first impression. Make it a good one. Many people won't read beyond the heading, but they may remember it if it's a good "sound byte." Headings should be brief, descriptive, and engaging. Don't underestimate the value of getting right to the point, but sometimes a longer heading or subheading is necessary to intrigue readers. Consider also using clever wordplay to intrigue or make your heading fun, but only if it represents your announcement well. If the fun heading isn't descriptive enough for your message and your audience, you might want to keep it simple.

The best headings usually:

- Are short
- Are informative
- Are descriptive
- Omit articles (*a*, *an*, *the*) unless they are essential
- Omit pronouns (*he*, *she*, *it*, etc.) unless they are essential
- Refer to the focal point of the message.

Also, state in the headline what the reader will gain by reading on. Even when the announcement is about your company, always imagine the reader scanning headings with "What's in it for me?" as a background question. "How To" and "Quick Tips" articles are always popular and are often forwarded. If your announcement is about a product or service that can make clients richer, happier, thinner, or more vibrant—then say so in your heading. These are potential results that draw attention.

However, be careful not to lie or oversell, making promises you cannot keep. In general, writing is stronger without qualifiers such as *may*, *could*, and *can*, but they are absolutely necessary if they keep a potential benefit from sounding like a solid claim that may *not* be true for everyone.

Use the headings that follow as ideas for structure and to see words that consistently capture attention. These may be used as templates as you practice and become more creative.

- "Why BBB Customers Are Getting Attention Online"
- "Learn How to Create Wealth—and Have Time to Enjoy It"
- "How to Find Great Deals Antiquing"
- "Why ACM Is Moving to Toronto"
- "The Secret to QTU's Success"
- "JBO Construction Building New Image"
- "Sharing the Wealth—WBC Goes Public"
- "FREE Subscription to the *Park Street Writer*!"
- "Announcing a New Risk-Free Rewards Program"
- "Are You Ready for a New Kind of Broker?"
- "Visit KiKi's Online Stores for a Virtual Bonanza of Great Buys!"
- "FREE! A New Event Planning Guide from Celebration Rentals"
- "Top 10 Tips for Finding Your Dream Home"
- "If You Hate Spam, You'll Love Our Software!"
- "Travel Host Wins Top Honors for Top Notch Service"
- "The Art of Influence: A Lecture with Noted Author Penny Wise"
- "Nutrition in Action: A Weeklong Simulcast Series"
- "Spot Free Announces New Nontoxic Line"
- "Web Deals Announces Year-End Clearance"

- "Are You Ready for the Holiday?"
- "Is Your Fad Diet Making You Fatter?"
- "New BOC Stores to Open in Las Vegas Casinos"
- "Family Business Goes Public: See How Grandma Betty's Linens Went from Knoxville to Wall Street"
- "Stakes Are High for New Pedico CEO"

5. Choose Power Words

We touch here on word choices and style, but keep in mind that in many of the announcements you write for the public—and even for your employees, who are your internal customers—phrases should involve all the pertinent facts. To make your phrases even stronger, use language that has some muscle to it and words that are unique.

- Use language with proven strength. Where do you find power words? Read announcements and see what gets your attention. Some words and phrases are standard attention-getters, such as *new, advanced, cutting-edge, moneymaking, proven results, win-win, money-back satisfaction guarantee, today only, exciting, intriguing, successful,* and *powerful.*
- Use language that's unique. As you write your announcements, think of the obvious, easy words, then pick up a thesaurus and see what other words might have more punch in their places. What words and phrases play on your company name? Whenever possible, choose words that add power and pizzazz to your announcements.

6. Use Perfect Quotes

Sometimes someone else has said exactly what you want to say. You may find a quote from a great leader whose name lends credibility to the statement. We've given some quotes and some ideas for where you might share quotes in the section "Message of the Day / Week / Month" in Chapter 6.

You also may want to quote those about whom you are writing. Quote the company sales manager, the customer, or your employee of the month to give press releases and articles stronger credibility and readability.

If you use quotes within text, vary the words you use to refer to the speaker to keep your writing fresh and interesting. Even slight variations make a big difference. To show how easy they can be, here are seventeen different ways to reference a quote within your text:

1. "... said MJB."
2. "... stated MJB."
3. "MJB added ..."
4. "... added MJB."
5. "... according to MJB."
6. "... concluded MJB."
7. "... announced MJB."
8. "MJB noted ..."
9. "... noted MJB."
10. "MJB emphasized ..."
11. "MJB commented ..."
12. "According to MJB ..."
13. "MJB responded ..."

14. "MJB's response was . . ."
15. "MJB announced . . ."
16. "MJB reported . . ."
17. "MJB replied . . ."

Perfect!

While you still have our *Perfect Phrase* library to consult, you are now also a *perfect phrase* generator—or well on your way to becoming one! Even if you have the perfect idea, remember that writing, editing, and proofreading are complex processes, and even the most well-intended phrase may need a little touch-up. As you read on, you'll learn some tips for doing so and some advice to always have someone else edit and proofread. Those, however, are last stages. Fear of a misplaced comma should never keep you from generating and writing down your own perfect phrases. *Write on!*

Chapter 13

Write On!

"The beautiful part of writing is that you don't have to get it right the first time, unlike, say, a brain surgeon."
—Robert Cromier

If you're creating an announcement that's more than a phrase or two, breaking the project into steps will help make the process more manageable and assure that you don't miss important final steps, such as proofreading. We recommend using a standard writing process, such as the following "Six Steps to Good Writing." Beyond these six steps, we recommend that you become familiar with some of the most common grammatical errors, such as "The Top Five Grammar Flubs" explained in this chapter. While they are often made, they're still not accepted as correct, and they will affect your image.

Also, announcements—especially brief ones—may be rushed out without a careful proofreading. But this final check before an announcement goes out is extremely important. After all, your image is no small thing. The last section of this chapter discusses why it is important that your proofreading go beyond spell-check and grammar-check.

Six Steps to Good Writing

For letters, press releases, and other announcements that are more than just a few lines, it's helpful to follow this simple six-step process:

1. **Plan.** Planned writing is easier writing.
2. **Outline.** Outlines give direction. They don't have to be formal—just road maps.
3. **Draft.** Write the draft without worrying about any rules. Just get words on paper.
4. **Edit.** Once the draft is complete, edit using guidelines for good grammar, usage, and strong writing.
5. **Rewrite.** Now, review and rewrite to ensure flow and consistency.
6. **Proofread.** Proofread word by word to catch errors in typing, spelling, or grammar.

After the piece has been refined and proofread, STOP. Many writers keep polishing until they wear out the perfectly polished piece.

Perfect Structure

When your announcement is more than a phrase, you'll want to craft your perfect phrases into perfect paragraphs. Limit paragraphs to five or six sentences. Reading seems to go more quickly when paragraphs are short. Begin paragraphs with topic sentences to give direction. User-friendly sentences are short, use powerful words, and eliminate unnecessary words and phrases.

The perfect structure for a perfect paragraph usually begins with your main point. Immediately state why you are writing. Don't keep your audience in suspense.

Follow with relevant details. Include facts that support the point you want to make. Let the reader know where you are going. If you plan to discuss three energy alternatives, say so. Don't keep them guessing.

Do what you can to simplify reading. Use subheads, proper capitalization, appropriate fonts, italics, bold, bullets, or space (not necessarily all in one piece). Use an appropriate subhead or phrase to indicate the conclusion. The perfect paragraph is clear, to the point, and easy to scan.

The Top Five Grammar Flubs

Following are five of the most common grammatical errors. Many people don't realize they need to know these rules because they use grammar-check software. Like spell-checkers, these programs are imperfect. Another reason people tend to make these errors in permanent, public announcements is that they think they know correct usage because they know what "sounds right." The problem is that misuse is so common that something may sound right because we've heard it used incorrectly so many times—even in advertising and on the news, and even from public speakers who are otherwise well spoken.

Proper usage is, however, the standard, and those who know will feel more confident about your company if you use language correctly. You can have a laid-back style, but you can be just as laid-back and still use correct grammar. Catchy announcements sometimes break the rules, but always know that you are breaking them and why. A few common errors that stand out and don't look like stylistic choices are errors involving pronoun choice, subject-verb agreement, descriptive words, tense, and parallel structure.

1. Pronoun Usage

Pronouns are often misused, but correct pronoun usage is an important detail that contributes to your professional image. For instance, many people think the pronouns *I, he,* and *she* are more generally correct than *me, him,* and *her,* but no pronoun is more proper in a general sense. Each has its place. *I, he, she, we,* and *they* are subject pronouns and should only be used when they are the subjects of sentences. *Me, him, her, us,* and *them* are object pronouns, used when they are the objects of sentences. (*You* is used as both subject and object.) Here are some examples: Joan and *I* (subject) went to the meeting. Elvira joined Joan and *me* (object).

2. Subject and Verb Agreement

Perfect phrases have perfect harmony, in which subjects and verbs agree. Confusion is common in many instances, such as when there are multiple subjects, plural and singular subjects combined, or phrases set off by commas. Consider the verb changes from *is* to *are* in the following sentences:

- "The entire QT team *is* grateful for your contribution." (*Team* is a singular word that treats the people at QT as a single group, so *is* is correct.)
- "The members of the QT team *are* grateful for your contribution." (Here, the subject is the team members

themselves rather than the team as a whole, requiring the plural *are*.)

■ "The QT Corporation CEO and the entire QT team *are* grateful for your contribution." (Here the CEO and the team are grouped as the subject—requiring the plural *are*.)

■ "QT Corporation's CEO, along with the entire team, *is* grateful for your contribution." (The subject is "QT Corporation's CEO," requiring *is*. The *team* is not part of the subject in this sentence because it is set off by commas. That makes *the entire team* a *parenthetical phrase* not essential to the sentence, so it is not part of the subject.)

If you want people to agree with your message, make sure your message agrees with itself!

3. Descriptive Words

Correct use of descriptive words can also be tricky. Following are some examples of correct usage that sometimes look wrong to people as incorrect usage becomes more common. In the first set of examples, the word *efficiently* is correct because it describes the action expressed by the verb *completes* (a *verb* expresses action; an *adverb* modifies a verb; the -*ly* ending is a cue that identifies adverbs).

■ "GEO *completes* estimates efficiently."
■ "GEO *completes* them more *efficiently* than the competition."
■ "GEO *completes* them *most efficiently*."

In the second set of examples, the word *efficient* is correct because it describes the noun *GEO* (a *noun* is a person, place, or thing; an *adjective* modifies a noun).

- "GEO *is efficient* with completing estimates."
- "GEO *is more efficient* than anyone else in the department."
- "GEO *is the most efficient.*"

4. Tense

Strong writing often uses the present tense. For example, "LOL Corp. cares about bringing smiles to children" is stronger than "LOL Corp. has always cared about bringing smiles to children." Strong writing is also consistent in time. Don't jump from one tense to another unless you are specifically marking a change in time. For instance, say, "Our winter sale starts today, and we're offering our lowest prices ever!" rather than "Our winter sale started today, and we'll offer our lowest prices ever!" Jumping around in tense not only causes your reader tension, it weakens your message.

5. Parallel Structure

Sentences that have parallel structure are not only grammatically correct, they also sound smoother and align your points to be easily seen and processed by those who read or scan your announcement. Compare the following two phrases:

- Great phrases have clarity, are concise, will be correct, and follow the lines of parallelism.
- Great phrases are clear, concise, correct, and parallel.

The second is more of all the things it says great sentences should be—and that makes it more eye-catching and easier to process and remember.

Here's another example of a sentence that's not parallel:

- Forman Co. selected Williams for the leadership role because of his clear vision, strong ethics, and he's shown positive results.

Here's the sentence with parallel structure:

- Forman Co. selected Williams for the leadership role because of his clear vision, strong ethics, and positive results.

Be creative in your words, ideas, placement, and tone, but keep your sentences in line with parallel structure.

Consider a Grammar Refresher Course

The information in this section may help you decide whether a grammar refresher course might be helpful to your business writing. Again, these are very common errors, so most people can use a refresher at some time. You also may want to consider, whether you alter our *perfect phrases* or write your own, if engaging the services of a professional editor could be well worth the cost for the payoff of a polished written image.

Translation Flubs

Whether you're writing your own announcement or slogan, using one from this book, or adapting a standard announcement from somewhere else, translate carefully when you go international! While we all make mistakes, we'd all rather learn from someone else's.

Following are some now-famous badly translated phrases that were meant to announce a great product and instead shocked and amused readers , as well as announced that these companies were careless in creating international announcements and campaigns:

- When the Coors slogan, "Turn It Loose" was translated into Spanish, the translation was read as "Suffer from Diarrhea."
- Colgate introduced a toothpaste in France called Cue, the name of a notorious porno magazine.
- An American T-shirt maker in Miami printed shirts for the Spanish market that promoted the Pope's visit. Instead of "I saw the Pope" (el Papa), the shirts read "I Saw the Potato" (la papa).
- The Dairy Association expanded the "Got Milk?" advertising campaign to Mexico, where the Spanish translation read "Are You Lactating?"
- General Motors had a tough time selling the Nova car in Central and South America, where "No va" (in Spanish) means "It Doesn't Go."
- Frank Perdue's chicken slogan, "It takes a strong man to make a tender chicken," was translated into Spanish as "it takes an aroused man to make a chicken affectionate."
- American Airlines advertised its new leather first-class seats in the Mexican market with its "Fly in Leather" campaign, which translated as "Fly Naked" (vuela en cuero) in Spanish.
- The Scandinavian vacuum manufacturer Electrolux didn't know American idioms when using this phrase in an American campaign: "Nothing Sucks like an Electrolux."

- When Gerber started selling baby food in Africa, it used the same packaging as in the United States, with the smiling baby on the label. Later it was learned that in Africa, companies routinely put pictures on the labels of what's inside because many people can't read.
- Pepsi's "Come Alive with the Pepsi Generation" translated into "Pepsi Brings Your Ancestors Back from the Grave" in Chinese.
- Clairol introduced the "Mist Stick," a curling iron, in Germany only to find out that "mist" is slang for manure.
- When Parker Pen marketed a ballpoint pen in Mexico, its ads were supposed to have read, "It won't leak in your pocket and embarrass you." The company thought that the word "embarazar" (to impregnate) meant to embarrass, so the ad read: "It won't leak in your pocket and make you pregnant."
- "Win a Milano Weekend!" This enticement to enter a contest for a vacation prize to Milan, Italy, was shown with an illustration of the Eiffel Tower in Paris, France.

Where did these companies go wrong? How can you avoid costly and embarrassing errors? Mistakes will happen, and even the best translator may not be perfect, but following the three basic guidelines below will give you the best chance for smooth translations that accurately represent your intended message:

- **Use a translation service that employs real people with whom you can communicate.** Online translators are risky. They don't have context or nuances. Your announcement could be translated with grammatical errors at best or laughable or offensive errors at worst.

- **Use translators who have knowledge of the context, culture, customs, and slang of the language to which you are translating.** You can easily offend or make your company the butt of a joke. You can also say something that is taboo or even the opposite of what you meant to say.
- **Use graphics that are accurate or culturally correct.** Again, your translator needs to be familiar with the culture, not just the language.

Grammar-Check, Spell-Check, and Human-Check

Always use spell-check, but *never* rely solely on it. Double check. Even for the briefest announcement, proofreading is the writer's most valuable asset. Read slowly, looking at each individual word as you read; read aloud; and get someone else to read what you've written as well. The best promotional piece or letter cannot do its job if it has even one grammatical error. That error can become a distraction, even a focus, for the reader, and your message can be lost.

You may be a great proofreader, but we all miss errors in our own work. When we read what we have written, we're too familiar with what we meant to write, so our eyes tend to see what we think we wrote and miss small errors that we would have easily seen in someone else's writing. *Always* have someone else read any announcement before it goes out. If you establish a process in which more than one other person proofreads each announcement, even better. That final check will help ensure that your *perfect phrases* are indeed perfect.

Conclusion

"Don't cry because it's over, smile because it happened."

—Dr. Seuss

B e visible to the public eye. In the name of your company, don't be shy. Publish, proclaim, report, broadcast, and blast. Communicate, circulate, advertise, and apprise. Disclose, divulge, reveal, or drop hints. Toot, trumpet, and tout. Be seen, be heard, be talked about! *Announce! Announce! Announce!*

If you've been inspired to find new ways and phrases to make announcements to clients, customers, investors, employees, or the world, then this conclusion is just the beginning. Announcements shouldn't be a passing thought or one that is with you only as you read this and not once you pick up the next book. Once you make writing announcements a daily, weekly, or monthly routine, you'll find that the people you address—both internal and external audiences—will not only feel more informed, they'll feel more connected to your business and invested in your success.

We wish you great visibility and success, and we look forward to hearing your announcements!

Resources

Other Helpful Perfect Phrase Books

- *Perfect Phrases for Sales Presentations*, Linda Eve Diamond, McGraw-Hill, 2009.
- *Perfect Phrases for Building Strong Teams*, Linda Eve Diamond, McGraw-Hill, 2007.
- *Perfect Phrases for Business Letters*, Ken O'Quinn, McGraw-Hill, 2005.
- *Perfect Phrases for Customer Service*, Robert Bacal, McGraw-Hill, 2005.
- *Perfect Phrases for Motivating and Rewarding Employees*, Harriet Diamond and Linda Eve Diamond, McGraw-Hill, 2005.

Grammar and Usage Resources

- *E-Z English*, fourth edition, Harriet Diamond and Phyllis Dutwin, Barron's Educational Series, Inc., 2009.
- *The Elements of Style: 50th Anniversary Edition*, William Strunk Jr. and E. B. White, Longman, 2008.
- *Executive Writing: American Style*, Linda Eve Diamond, Marsha Fahey, and Harriet Diamond, Apocryphile Press, 2007.
- *Grammar in Plain English*, fourth edition, Harriet Diamond and Phyllis Dutwin, Barron's Educational Series, Inc., 2005.

About the Authors

Linda Eve Diamond is the author of several books in the areas of education, self-help, motivation, team building, business writing, and poetry. Listening as a critical, learnable skill is a central theme throughout her diverse works. After writing and teaching communication skills in a corporate training setting for nearly fifteen years, she decided to fine-tune her focus on communication by exploring the importance of listening—from the inner to the interpersonal—as essential for personal fulfillment and business success.

Linda is the recipient of two 2008 International Listening Association Awards: the President's Award and the award for Listening in the Business Sector. Also an award-winning poet, Linda shares her perspective on the art of listening through her creative works as well. She is available for speaking engagements and listening skills training that focuses on the power of listening in all contexts—from personal relationships to business success to listening issues within the healthcare industry. Listening skills training can be customized to any organization or group.

Visit Linda Eve Diamond's regularly updated websites at http://LindaEveDiamond.com and http://ListenersUnite.com.

Harriet Diamond is the author of several books in the areas of business and education. She retired in 2004 from running Diamond Associates, a training and consulting firm she established in 1985. She and the talented team she assembled, which included her daughter and coauthor, Linda Eve Diamond, created and delivered training programs and provided consulting services in a number of areas, including the pharmaceutical, manufacturing, healthcare, financial, transportation, and hospitality industries.

During her years as a business owner, Harriet held leadership positions in the New Jersey Association of Women Business Owners, the Union County Private Industry Council (now Workforce Development Board), and the Union County Chamber of Commerce. She also was an active member of the New Jersey Board of Public Utilities' Supplier Diversity Development Council, the Women Presidents' Organization, the Union County Chamber of Commerce, the Westfield Chamber of Commerce, and the Atlantic City Chamber of Commerce. She was the New Jersey Association of Women Business Owners' Business Woman of the Year in 1995 and the recipient of three New Jersey Institute of Technology New Jersey Author Awards and a New Jersey Senate citation for Outstanding Contributions to Adult Education. Harriet is now active in her new community, Atlantic City, New Jersey, assisting small businesses and community organizations. Visit Harriet at http://harrietdiamond.net.

Harriet and **Linda Eve Diamond** have also coauthored *Perfect Phrases for Motivating and Rewarding Employees*, McGraw-Hill, 2005, and *Teambuilding That Gets Results*, Sourcebooks, 2007.

The Right Phrase for Every Situation...Every Time

Perfect Phrases for Building Strong Teams
Perfect Phrases for Business Letters
Perfect Phrases for Business Proposals and Business Plans
Perfect Phrases for Business School Acceptance
Perfect Phrases for College Application Essays
Perfect Phrases for Cover Letters
Perfect Phrases for Customer Service
Perfect Phrases for Dealing with Difficult People
Perfect Phrases for Dealing with Difficult Situations at Work
Perfect Phrases for Documenting Employee Performance Problems
Perfect Phrases for Executive Presentations
Perfect Phrases for Landlords and Property Managers
Perfect Phrases for Law School Acceptance
Perfect Phrases for Lead Generation
Perfect Phrases for Managers and Supervisors
Perfect Phrases for Managing Your Small Business
Perfect Phrases for Medical School Acceptance
Perfect Phrases for Meetings
Perfect Phrases for Motivating and Rewarding Employees
Perfect Phrases for Negotiating Salary & Job Offers
Perfect Phrases for Perfect Hiring
Perfect Phrases for the Perfect Interview
Perfect Phrases for Performance Reviews
Perfect Phrases for Real Estate Agents & Brokers
Perfect Phrases for Resumes
Perfect Phrases for Sales and Marketing Copy
Perfect Phrases for the Sales Call
Perfect Phrases for Setting Performance Goals
Perfect Phrases for Small Business Owners
Perfect Phrases for the TOEFL Speaking and Writing Sections
Perfect Phrases for Writing Grant Proposals
Perfect Phrases in American Sign Language for Beginners
Perfect Phrases in French for Confident Travel
Perfect Phrases in German for Confident Travel
Perfect Phrases in Italian for Confident Travel
Perfect Phrases in Spanish for Confident Travel to Mexico
Perfect Phrases in Spanish for Construction
Perfect Phrases in Spanish for Gardening and Landscaping
Perfect Phrases in Spanish for Household Maintenance and Child Care
Perfect Phrases in Spanish for Restaurant and Hotel Industries

Visit mhprofessional.com/perfectphrases for a complete product listing.

Learn more. Mc Graw Hill Do more.